John Wesley Haley and Building the Indigenous Church

John Wesley Haley and Building the Indigenous Church

Reflections on Self-Determination in Twentieth Century Burundi

Edited by John McCready

John Wesley Haley and Building the Indigenous Church

Copyright © John McCready. All rights reserved.

Published 2015 by Clements Publishing, Toronto, ON

www.clementspublishing.com

Cover design by Lisa Howden

Includes bibliographical references

ISBN 978-1-926798-71-4

Contents

Foreword	vii
Introduction	1
1. Haley: A Man Before His Time *Burton Hamilton*	11
2. The Manuscript *John Wesley Haley*	59
3. The Indigenous Church in Burundi *Deogratias Nshimiyimana, Evariste Harerimana, Desire Mpfubusa*	135
4. The Mission Temporary, The Church Permanent *Dan Sheffield*	155
Notes on Haley's Journal	205
Select Bibliography	209

Foreword

Howard Snyder [1]

Missionary pioneer John Wesley Haley is timely and prophetic today because of the way he conjoined theory and practice in pioneering deep church planting in Central Africa—and reflected on this in his writings.

I therefore commend this volume and welcome it as a significant contribution to contemporary debates about and contemplated strategies for evangelism, church planting, and the nature of Christian mission.

Today the term "indigenous church" is often easily dismissed because the term is not as current in missiological debates as it once was. Yet the underlying issue is indeed very current: How are faithful, fruitful, and enduring churches established within particular cultural contexts? And how does that relate to the larger *missio Dei*, the mission of God?

Haley (appropriately named John Wesley Haley) was a church planter who learned from experience, from Scripture, from history, but also from contemporary writings on mission history and strategy. As this book documents, Haley had read and fully digested Anglican missionary Roland Allen's highly influential 1912 book, *Missionary Methods: St. Paul's or Ours?* Presumably he also read Allen's later book *The Spontaneous Expansion of the Church*. And he read much else besides. He was aware of Presbyterian missionary John

---

1. Author of *The Problem of Wineskins, Community of the King, Salvation Means Creation Healed*, and other books, Howard A. Snyder currently serves as Visiting Director of the Manchester Wesley Research Centre in Manchester, England.

Nevius' work in China and Korea and of the "Nevius Plan" for starting indigenous churches. As noted in this book, Haley wrote in 1932, "I think all our missionaries should read [Charles Allen Clark's] *The Korean Church and the Nevius Methods* and the new missionaries should pass an examination on it. Then the reading course should include such books as [Roland Allen's] *Missionary Methods: St Paul's or Ours?* and a number of other such books."

Haley was in touch with the best and most forward-looking literature about missions in his day.

Because of John Wesley Haley's accomplishments, his insights, and his clear articulation of fundamental biblical principles about the church and its contextualized expansion, this book has particular relevance today.

Introduction

John McCready [1]

John Wesley Haley (1878-1951) was a Canadian who served as a Free Methodist Church missionary in Portuguese East Africa (Mozambique) and South Africa (1902 to 1934). While in South Africa, he had a calling to head "north" and a vision for Central Africa. At the age of 56, John Wesley Haley and his wife, Jennie (Hamilton) Haley, started as the first Free Methodist Church missionaries in Burundi (1935 to 1946). John Wesley Haley wrote two books on his work in Africa: *Life in Mozambique and South Africa* (1926) and *But Thy Right Hand* (1949).

At the heart of this book is a manuscript on building the indigenous church that was written by John Wesley Haley. Following forty-four years as a missionary in Africa, John Wesley Haley was working on this previously unpublished manuscript at the time of his death.

John Wesley Haley developed this manuscript on the indigenous church based on extraordinary Christian devotion and commitment, unusual powers of observation and understanding, and tremendous experience and accomplishment. Beyond the Bible, John Wesley Haley was an astute observer and a reader. John Wesley Haley read

---

1. Dr. John McCready of Healthy Horizons Consulting has worked in community development and applied research throughout his career. In reconnecting with Burundi, he has become a Visiting Professor at Hope Africa University and the founder and director of the Haley McCready Outreach and Development Fund (see http://haleymccreadyfund.com).

material about missionary theory and methods. In his foreword to the manuscript, he makes direct reference to Roland Allen and his book *Missionary Methods: St. Paul's or Ours?* (1912). A number of times, Haley refers to the three major, critical principles that underpin the building of an indigenous church: self-support, self-propagation and self-governance.

When John Wesley Haley arrived in Urundi in 1934 (now Burundi) and started his work at Muyebe in 1935, he was intent on building an indigenous church but, as he admitted, he did not know how he was going to do so. He found the answer and he did an amazing job of building an indigenous church. From nothing, John Wesley Haley built an indigenous church in Burundi that after only twenty years was the largest Free Methodist Church conference in the world (i.e., the conference with the most members). Today, there are no permanent Free Methodist Church missionaries in Burundi and the Free Methodist Church of Burundi has far more members (155,207) than Canada and the United States combined.

Critics have linked missionary work with colonization. It is important to note that John Wesley Haley appears to have been critical of colonialism and, when practised by missionaries, critical of the church. John Wesley Haley had an understanding of the political and economic context in Africa and the importance of self-determination for the African people. He points to situations where the Africans resisted colonization and pursued development on their own. In an uncanny fashion, John Wesley Haley suggests that without an indigenous church, missionaries could be forced out if war broke out and the church would falter if the indigenous people were not developing their own church. The indigenous Free Methodist Church in Burundi, Rwanda and the Democratic Republic of Congo has endured terrible wars and the withdrawal of missionaries but the indigenous Free Methodist Church continues to grow in these countries.

John Wesley Haley was not the first person to discover the idea of building an indigenous church but he was at the cutting edge of attempting to build an indigenous church. On his own, he learned how to build an indigenous church and he did so very successfully. He stands apart from others by having successfully developed an indigenous church and his legacy lives on in Central Africa. John Wesley Haley's manuscript anchors missionary work in the Biblical model, highlights the essential principles of building an indigenous church and, through his experience, describes the implementation methods for ensuring self-determination; self-support, self-propagation and self-government.

From his missionary experience in South Africa and Mozambique, John Wesley Haley had come to understand that the best way, a more ethical way for the missionary work to be done was for the missionaries to look after themselves, treat the indigenous people as equals and respect the indigenous culture. Right from the beginning of building the indigenous church, the missionaries would train the indigenous people to be their own leaders, enable the indigenous people to pursue their own outreach and development and enable the indigenous people to build their own schools and churches and govern their own affairs and organizations.

John Wesley Haley went to South Africa in 1902 and was joined by Esther Jane Hamilton in 1905. They were married and had four children. He moved to Burundi in 1934 and was joined by his wife, Jennie Haley, and two daughters, Dorothy (20) and Peace Haley (16) at Muyebe on July 16, 1935. Dorothy took on office work and the schools and Peace ran the dispensary; the Morning Glory Clinic. Later, Dorothy Haley married Burton McCready and they became missionaries in Burundi (1940 to 1956) and, likewise, Peace

Haley married Oddvar Berg and they became missionaries in Burundi (1943 to 1958).

All four of the McCready children were born in Burundi and the McCready family returned to North America in 1956. John McCready, the editor of this book and the Haley manuscript, is the grandson of John Wesley Haley and Jennie (Hamilton) Haley and the son of Dorothy (Haley) McCready and Burton McCready.

I obtained my undergraduate degree at Spring Arbor College (1968) and moved to Canada where I acquired graduate and postgraduate degrees at the University of Toronto, studying community development and social policy in the Faculty of Social Work. I have had a career in what could generally be called community development work. In the last number of years, I have worked extensively with the indigenous people of Canada; Indians, Inuit and Métis. In Canada, the indigenous people clearly understand the impact of colonization and the importance of self-determination. It is satisfying to me to note that my grandfather understood these things before 1935. Moreover, it is impressive to me that my grandfather was able to encourage, promote and infuse self-support, self-propagation and self-government into the development of the church and education and health services.

I inherited the Haley and McCready papers. I knew that my grandfather had been writing a manuscript on the indigenous church at the time of his death but it was not included in the papers I acquired from the McCready family home in Spring Arbor, Michigan. I had started to accept that the manuscript was lost. I made yet another trip to the Maple Grove Christian Retreat Centre in Thamesford, Ontario, Canada (formerly the Free Methodist Church Camp for the West Ontario Conference; the home Conference of the Haley's and McCready's). I spoke to Doris Withenshaw, lead volunteer for the Robb Free Methodist Historical Centre at the time, and, eventually, she handed me a couple of files that contained the manuscript. Apparently, my mother, Dorothy (Haley) McCready, had given the manuscript, along with some other materials, to the Historical Centre. I felt so fortunate to find the manuscript, gain full access to it and have the opportunity to have it considered for publication.

In doing the editing, considerable effort was made to produce the manuscript that John Wesley Haley intended. The manuscript was not finished and, through its notes, organization and repetition, the slightly edited version in this book retains some of the characteristics of an unfinished piece of work. The wording, writing style and punctuation were for the most part retained, even when it was difficult. A few commas were added when it seemed necessary to aid the reader's understanding; particularly, when the sentences were very lengthy. Although the author used feminine pronouns in reference to the church, he used masculine pronouns for the missionary workers. Noting that John Wesley Haley supported the active involvement of female missionaries, the masculine references were retained.

In many cases, the references were not provided. The editor attempted to find the references and a bibliography was developed and included with this version of the manuscript. The author used the King James Version of the Bible and he may have been working from the 1917 edition of the Scofield Reference Bible. To respect the author and the time of the writing, the King James Version quotations were retained. All but one of the references was identified. A few footnotes are provided in order to provide the reader with explanations.

The manuscript was not complete and so there was no summary at the end. To serve as a summary and concluding chapter, permission was sought and received to include a presentation and article by author; John Wesley Haley. The final chapter succinctly puts the whole the story back together.

The project of getting the manuscript published was not accomplished without the critical involvement of others. I would like to thank my mother, Dorothy (Haley) McCready, for preserving the manuscript and I am very grateful to Doris Withenshaw who was very helpful, patient and generous in my persistent pursuit of the manuscript and other materials.

When I found the manuscript, the first thing I did was to ask Howard Snyder to review it. He reviewed the manuscript, indicated that it should be published and introduced me to Rob Clements of Clements Publishing Group Inc. I am particularly grateful to Janet Hamilton who prepared a Word file of the manuscript and Burton Hamilton, my distant cousin on my maternal grandmother's side; Jennie (Hamilton) Haley, who provided support, encouragement, advice and guidance in editing and seeking a publisher. Throughout the book development process, our contributors have received tremendous support in the form of background information and photographs from Susan Panak, Acquisitions and Archives, Spring Arbor University and Cathy Robling, Marston Memorial Historical Center, Free Methodist Church – USA.

In exploring the publishing possibilities, Burton Hamilton and I learned that in publishing size matters. On its own, the manuscript was thought to be more of a lengthy pamphlet than a book. I soon began to consider additional complementary writing contributions that would produce a much more complete story.

The first contribution to the book, *Haley: A Man Before His Time*, was written by Rev. Burton Hamilton who certainly rose to the occasion and masterfully describes the man and his work. As a boy, Burton Hamilton knew John Wesley Haley from visits to the Hamilton home. Burton Hamilton insisted on reviewing primary sources. His knowledge and description of the historical Canadian context and his writing style provide an accessible and interesting picture of Haley's life and times and character. By relying on and extensively quoting from the detailed journals that John Wesley Haley left behind, Burton Hamilton's description of the man and his work has an autobiographical characteristic, adding special interest and authenticity.

The next part of the book is the Haley manuscript on building the indigenous church and it is followed by an update or status report on the current indigenous Free Methodist Church of Burundi. Fittingly, the update on the indigenous Free Methodist Church of Burundi was written by indigenous members of the indigenous Church; Bishop Déogratias Nshimiyimana, Rev. Evariste Harerimana and Rev. Désiré Mpfubusa. Convincingly, the update indicates that the large and growing indigenous Church remains self-supporting, self-propagating and self-governing. This section of the book was made possible by Burton Hamilton acquiring donations from generous members of the Hamilton Family who gave a sufficient amount of money to provide enough research assistance to allow the bishop to be the senior author.

The concluding part of this book, *The Mission Temporary, The Church Permanent*, was written by Rev. Dan Sheffield, Director of Global and Intercultural Ministries for the Free Methodist Church in Canada, who takes a scholarly approach to much of his work and has numerous other publications. One of his desires has been to promote the heritage of Canadian contributors to the growth of The Free Methodist Church around the world. Dan Sheffield reviews John Wesley Haley's model for building the indigenous church within its international mission context, explaining what was going on at the time. He knowledgeably and insightfully identifies the people, the writings and the ideas that influenced Haley's indigenous church-building approach and examines its meaning for the present context. Dan

Sheffield graciously offered and completed the "typesetting" for the book and The Free Methodist Church in Canada generously contributed some of his time and some of the publishing expenses.

Editing this book has been only one of my activities in reconnecting with my rich family heritage and my beloved Burundi. I have taught Community Needs Assessment at Hope Africa University. I have established the Haley McCready Outreach and Development Fund, A Living Memorial (see http://haleymccreadyfund.com).

The two-fold purpose of the Haley McCready Outreach and Development Fund is (1) to keep alive the memory and service contributions of early missionaries John Wesley and Jennie (Hamilton) Haley and Burton and Dorothy (Haley) McCready and, most importantly, (2) to keep alive the legacy of outreach to and development of the indigenous people of Burundi. The Haley McCready Fund provides small grants to students and graduates of Hope Africa University who design and implement development projects with indigenous, needy beneficiaries. Relying on donations from generous people like you, the Haley McCready Fund has been able to provide funding for 12 projects and approved funding for three more. Although expected to be very small, all of the royalties from the sale of this book will be given directly to the Haley McCready Outreach and Development Fund for continuing direct investment into outreach and the development of the indigenous people of Burundi.

Dr John McCready with Rev Matayo Myiruko, a respected leader in the Free Methodist Church in Burundi. John asked him what he remembered most about John Wesley Haley and he said emphatically, "He really loved people."

1

Haley: A Man Before His Time

Burton Hamilton

Burton Hamilton [1]

At Haley's memorial service, Byron S. Lamson, General Missionary Secretary of the Free Methodist Church, gave the following tribute:

> Mr. Haley had an unlimited faith in God. His dependence on prayer was great... He had a great supply of courage and moral daring....He represented the Missionary Board at great conferences in Africa, United States and Canada.... His books and magazine articles were read beyond the denomination. He was the first chairman of the Protestant Alliance in Ruanda-Urundi, where Baptists, Friends, Methodists, Anglicans and others testified to his spiritual influence.[2]

Gerald Bates, author of a biography *Soul Afire* about Haley, wrote:

> Somewhere there should be a statue of John Wesley

---

1. Burton Hamilton has served as pastor and youth worker, high school counsellor, founding principal of a Christian day school, and interim seminary president. He has served on many committees and boards. As he says, "God has given me a wonderful ride in this life!"
2. *The Missionary Tidings*, April 15, 1951.

Haley with a Bible in one hand and the other shading his eyes and looking northward. A great part of his career was going northward, into Burundi, northward into Rwanda. Haley was the principal founder of arguably the greatest mission initiative in Free Methodist history in terms of fruitfulness.[3]

John Wesley Haley was a man after God's own heart. Thousands of his spiritual descendants rise up and call him blessed today. And many more have died with his praise on their lips.

Such high praise causes the reader to wonder what factors shaped the life of this man. One would be tempted to guess that he had been born into very favourable circumstances, and that he lacked nothing in opportunities and education. But such was not the case.

Early Years

John Wesley Haley, was the fifth of seven children born to Hiram W. Haley and Catherine (Black)[4] Haley. The senior Haleys had moved from Hastings County in rural Ontario, Canada, to the Bracebridge area of the same province, to take up Free Grants of Land first offered in 1868. The 1881 census lists Haley as two years of age.[5]

Ruth Holtz, Reference Librarian of the Bracebridge Public Library describes the Bracebridge area in 1878. "*Guidebook and Atlas of Muskoka and Parry Sound* shows H. W. Haley located on Concession 2 Macaulay Township, close to the boundary with Draper Township. The family would

---

3. *Free Methodist Historical Society Newsletter*, Summer 2001, Vol. 2, No. 1.
4. Some census documents list the family name as Black – some as Blake. The fact that their son was named Blake may decide in favour of the name Blake.
5. Canada Census, 1881.

likely have been served by the Post Office at the home of George Gregg of Monsell, a settlement which has since been completely erased. The children may have attended a one room school nearby but located in the next township.

"Muskoka was a brand new area opened for settlement with Free Grants of Land in 1868. In those early days, settlers endured an arduous journey using a combination of stage and steamboat to arrive at the North Falls on the Muskoka River, which later developed into the town of Bracebridge. By 1871, the village of Bracebridge had 4 hotels, 7 stores, 2 sawmills, a grist mill, 2 bakeries, 2 butcher shops, a sash and door factory, blacksmith shop, cabinet warehouse, drug store, book store, court house, crown lands office, registry office, jail, printing office, churches, schools, Orange Hall, and Post Office with daily mail service.

"Early economic history of the area involved trapping, lumbering and tanneries. Although early settlers claimed land hoping to farm, much of the land proved to be ill suited to agriculture.

"In 1878, the year of Mr. Haley's birth, the village of Bracebridge, a good distance from the Haley home, but certainly the nearest community of any size, had grown to the point of supporting 2 newspapers.

"Life for these early settlers of Muskoka was indeed difficult. The growing season was short and the soil not as fertile as expected, but they did plant crops of peas, oats wheat and potatoes. Each family kept a large vegetable garden, planted strawberries and apple trees. They also turned to the natural crops of the area, picking wild berries and making maple syrup.

"Many of the men would work in the lumber mills all winter and in the spring some would also work at peeling hemlock to supply tanbark for the nearby tanneries. Of course, everyone would also have to cut their own supply of firewood to keep the fires burning at home all year.

"People walked farther than we would think to do today to visit neighbours, attend church and buy supplies. They also travelled by horse and buggy or horse and sleigh, depending on the season.

"Illness and injury were always present due to the harsh and often dangerous work and the scarcity of medical help."[6]

Another writer, Rev. C. H. Sage, who had been appointed by the North Michigan Conference of the Free Methodist Church to open work in Canada, described the country, "with its granite rocks, pine stumps and summer frosts, as the worst he had ever seen for making a living. He went on to explain that the government had stripped the valuable timber and then had advertised 200 acres of free land to settlers."[7]

Perhaps because of the unsuitability of the land around Bracebridge for farming, the family moved to Thornyhurst, in Sombra Township[8]. Records are unclear about the date of this removal to Sombra. However, a story told to the writer by his grandfather would indicate that some of Haley's early education took place at Thornyhurst. Gramp's story goes something like this:

> "We were playing ball in the schoolyard. I got tired of waiting for John to 'step up' to the plate, so I snatched the bat away from him and took his place at bat. John began to cry. I felt terrible, and always wondered if he ever forgave me for that."[9]

---

6. Communication received from Ms. Holz of the Bracebridge Public Library.
7. John Wilkins Sigsworth, *The Battle Was the Lord's*, Winona Lake: Light and Life Publishers, 1960, 70, 75.
8. Sombra Township lies between Sarnia and Wallaceburg, Ontario
9. This story was told to the author during one of the "too many" times that he was sent to the field to hoe sugar beets with his grandfather.

Evidently, all was forgiven. The two men and their wives took a vacation together to Florida in later years. In those 1880s Haley would have needed to go to Sarnia – 30 miles away, or Wallaceburg – 10 miles from home, to complete his high school education. This would probably necessitate his boarding in one of those places. Such was still the case when the writer's mother, living on the farm in Charlemont some thirty-five or forty years later, boarded in Wallaceburg during the week to attend high school.

Life in Sombra Township in the '80s, though somewhat different, was just as hard for the Haley family as it had been in Muskoka. David Allan tells of sending a local preacher from Charlemont to Thornyhurst to hold Sunday services, perhaps even for the Haley family. At the end of the Charlemont service, Allan found Local Preacher Josephus Harris standing at the Charlemont church door. "Brother Harris said they had to turn and come back and had hard work to make home. I said, 'A preacher is not supposed to turn back but to keep going as far as he can and then unhitch and if he cannot make it on horseback, tie his horse to the fence and make it through on foot, and never disappoint a congregation.' Brother Harris said, 'Brother Allan, it was no use, we could not make it in time for the service. We had a terrible time getting as far as we did and then getting back. The wheels filled with mud and would not go round and it took us half of our time punching mud out of the wheels, we were afraid it would twist the axle.'"[10]

Early Free Methodism in Canada

It is important to note that the genius of early Methodism in both the United States and Canada had been the Revival

---

10. David Allan, *From the Lumber Camp to the Ministry*, Toronto: Evangelical Publishers, 1938, 77.

Meeting. These had largely died out in that communion, but the newly formed Canadian Free Methodist Church now began to utilize such meetings very effectively. Services would go on night after night for many weeks – one reported as "dry" until a "break" in the sixth week, which precipitated continuation of a further eight weeks of meetings.[11] One of these revivals took place at Keith (later called Charlemont) in 1889-90.[12] Charlemont was dubbed the "Bee Hive" since many little societies hived off from this revival.

Following the Methodist tradition, Quarterly and District Meetings were held in the area. People from the surrounding areas would travel to the supporting society to spend the weekend in official meetings and more revival services. This provided an opportunity for fellowship, and for young people to become acquainted with each other. It is probable that John and his future bride became interested in each other during one of these events.

The camp meeting was another feature of this early church life. Camp Meetings had begun in the early eighteen hundreds among the Presbyterians of Kentucky. What had happened there in Kentucky, happened again among Free Methodists in Canada. People "were looking for a rare chance to hobnob with neighbours unseen for a year at a stretch. They hoped for entertainment in the form of rousing sermons, and a chance to let out feelings that were cramped up"[13] by a very harsh, often lonely, and pedestrian lifestyle. Such gatherings also provided sport for rowdies in the neighbourhood to do what they could to interrupt these meetings, (the only other amusements being cards, dances, drinking and the lodge.) It was at such a camp meeting on

---

11. Sigsworth, 27.
12. Ibid., 27.
13. Bernard A. Weisberger, *They Gathered at the River*, Boston: Little, Brown and Co., 1958, 26.

his father's farm, that John Haley's life would forever be changed.

A Cataclysmic Experience

The record of John Wesley Haley, his life and on-going education, is little known until the year 1898. This was a pivotal year in his life, for it was in this year, at a camp meeting held in the bush on his father's farm, that John became converted.[14] As his son-in-law Burton McCready wrote, "Having taken the first step, he never looked back. The victory of that day led him to join forces with the Free Methodist Church on probation and six months later in full connection. On July 22nd he was sanctified and in September was elected Sunday School Superintendent [of the Thornyhurst Church]. In 1899 he was granted [an] Exhorter's Licence, and in 1901 he was granted a Local Preacher's Licence."[15]

Haley would have been required to answer appropriately the 1891 Book of Discipline questions put to those who felt that they were called to preach, namely:

> "Do they know God as a pardoning God? Have they the love of God abiding in them? Do they desire nothing but God? And are they holy in all manner of conversation?
>
> Have they gifts (as well as grace) for the work? Have they (in some tolerable degree) a clear, sound understanding, a right judgement in the things of God, a just conception of salvation by faith? And has God given them any degree of utterance? Do they speak justly, readily, clearly?

---

14. Allan, 78.
15. McCready Papers. This is a collection of several folders of papers retained by John McCready

Have they fruit? Are any truly convinced of sin, and converted to God by their preaching?"[16]

Haley would also be required to engage faithfully in the four-year course of study laid out for preachers who desired to be ordained as Elders.[17] What Weisberger had observed about earlier Methodist preachers applied to Haley, Allan and others of their time; "Their preaching might be foolishness to some, but their audiences suffered them gladly...they spread the potent, pervasive, democratic and irresistible Arminian theology ...and it was to be the hallmark of revival preaching ever after. Because their lack of education made them laymen in all but name, they had proved by their work that they could be the backbone of evangelism."[18]

June 12, 1900, life began to change rapidly for Haley. The West Ontario Conference of the Free Methodist Church appointed him to assist Rev. W. H. Wilson who was pioneering in Western Canada. "Cheerfully and uncomplainingly he put up with the hardships which were incident to a new country and rigorous climate. He worked there successfully but his consecration [would lead] him farther than that. The first year God gave him a gracious revival at Caron, a small Prairie town, and from that revival came eighteen converts who formed the nucleus of the Westview Circuit."[19]

To Africa

Still a young, unmarried man, because of that deep consecration noted above, he felt the call to apply for missionary work in Africa. Accordingly, he was appointed as

---

16. *Discipline of the Free Methodist Church*, 1891, 48-49.
17. Ibid., 138-139.
18. Weisberger, 49.
19. McCready Papers.

the first Canadian missionary of the Free Methodist Church – assigned to South Africa. He sailed for Mozambique in 1902.

In 1905, "as previously arranged,"[20] Jennie Esther Hamilton arrived from Wilkesport, Ontario to become John Haley's bride. They had probably met at one of the many camp or quarterly meetings.

Consider the devotion and bravery of a twenty-eight year old woman making her way unattended from the backwoods of Ontario, through New York City, sailing off to the unknown challenges that awaited her! Very often, the spouse of an important individual is placed in the background. As was the case with John, we have nothing about Jennie's early life. We do know that she was the daughter of Jacob Hamilton. Brothers Jacob and Robert had both been converted and been granted Local Preacher Licences. They and their families had moved to Wilksport, Sombra Township, from Hastings County at about the same time as the Haley family had moved to the Thornyhurst area from Muskoka. In one of the many revival services held in the general area, Jacob had felt the call to preach,[21] and so had been assigned to the Wilkesport society.

"Jennie" (Esther Jane) Hamilton too, had left all to serve the Lord in South Africa. Interestingly, whether by mission or government dictate, John and Jennie completed an Anti-Nuptial Agreement in Durban, South Africa, prior to their marriage.[22]

---

20. Ibid.
21. Allan, 84.
22. McCready papers.

Haley's with baby Florence, ca. 1906.

Home life and travelling from station to station at considerable distance, often on foot, was hard, as was childbirth and care, often without assistance. To the union between John and Jennie on January 6, 1906 a daughter Florence was born. Haley's *Journal* recounts a series of several times when Florence was placed in the care of the Ryffs, missionaries in Germiston because of health and schooling concerns, and the unsuitability and demands of the situations in which the Haleys were placed. His *Journal* record bears testimony to the heartbreak that this caused for Jennie and him. "We have missed Florence very much, but have enjoyed immensely the long letters Mrs. Ryff has written about her, and the Lord has given 'more grace.'"[23]

Although Haley does not complain about them, those years in South Africa were very difficult ones for the Haleys. We see that they began to suffer debilitating health problems. "A severe cough had taken hold upon me, and I had no strength left. My Doctor said I was in the first stage of

23. J W Haley, *Journal*, page 36.

consumption, and as my head also troubled me we began to prepare to leave Inhambane."[24] "Mrs Haley began to have fever. She had attack after attack with vomiting spells and became so weak and reduced in flesh that I had to take her away... [She] had fever all the way down the coast and was so weak that she could only walk a few rods.[25]

It would seem from his *Journal* that the only medical assistance came from the use of quinine and some "powders," considered to be anti-inflammatories. However, the use of quinine had undesirable effects that may have contributed to the doctor's recommendation for a furlough and to "get on the land."[26] August 15, 1908, Haley writes, "Florence is having fever again. This is the first she has had for two months."[27] In spite of these challenges, Haley would write, "God's ways are best, and if we are worn out in God's work, we are not tired of it."[28] While preparing to sail for Canada, Haley also took out a life insurance policy on himself. "My reason for insuring is that I am fast growing old and cannot hope to live to be an old man if I stay at Inhambane. I am unable to save anything out of my salary as living is so high in Africa. My wife and child will need something if they should be left alone, and as this is an honest way of providing for them I felt it my duty to insure."[29]

At this point, the Mission Board, "granted us a furlough...and having fears of my health sent the money for our fares to us..."[30] Haley's hopes for the furlough were that "this year be a year of receiving. Receiving both spiritual

24. Ibid., 94.
25. Ibid., 95.
26. Ibid., 95.
27. Ibid., 93.
28. Ibid., 99.
29. Ibid., 107.
30. Ibid., 99.

and temporal wisdom and strength, that we may better serve Him in this land of sin when we return refreshed should Jesus tarry. Our aim is not so much to do when we return to our homeland, but to rest."[31]

Accordingly, the Haleys sailed for Canada February 25, 1909.[32] They arrived in Sarnia, at his mother's home, on April 13 – his conclusion, "the best of the journey is getting home!"[33] As his health allowed, they visited around the churches in Southern Ontario but on July 13 headed for Western Canada.

Back in Canada

Life on the Prairie was filled with one challenge after another. The Haleys attended a camp meeting that July, in Saskatchewan, where he was able to renew acquaintance with Free Methodists that he had known in 1902. We will let him tell the story: "The camp meeting was hard on me after the long trip and I was glad when it was over…we went to Rob Wilson's. They put up a tent for us to live in and gave me cream to drink and we visited around. We had a splendid time, but I found the visiting to be very hard on me."[34]

> "The conviction grew on me that I would not be well enough to go back to Africa for several years. I did not get strong and the sun hurt my head. I could not read more than two minutes without distress in my eyes and head. I could only write one or two letters at a time and deep thinking hurt me. My mind had been directed toward homesteading as I sailed from

31. Ibid., 101.
32. Ibid., 106.
33. Ibid., 111.
34. Ibid., 96.

Africa...I consulted my brethren in the ministry and in the laity, and all thought that as I was so broken in health and mentally tired that it would be the best thing I could do."[35]

"I secured for myself 640 acres, being Section 23, Township 12, Range 8 West of the 3rd Meridian....I got a horse from Brother Tanner and one from Rob Wilson and a wagon from Herbert Nesbitt and expected to start off alone but just the day before I was to start God gave me a helper in the person of John Brown....On Monday I went to Moose Jaw for lumber...surely God has chosen our inheritance...
"We put up a tent, found water in a little creek and dug beside it and got drinking water...I went to Morse for lumber...we started the shack 14 X 22 ft...our order from Eatons [Department Store] of household effects and supplies had come, so I sent for my wife to come. It was a lovely day and we suffered not although we were all day on the way in November. It was the last nice day we had for weeks. Another mercy God gave us. We slept in the tent, but the next day John and I got the shack so we could move in by nine at night."[36]

Later in 1909,

"[John] was returning from Morse, accompanied by Alfred Hicks, when 16 miles from home, a blizzard came on. We hurried along as fast as we could but finally it got so thick that at times we couldn't see the horses' heads. We finally got out, took the

---

35. Ibid., 116.
36. Ibid., 120

> halters in our hands and led the team…I never could have got home but for the Providential lull in the storm. My wife could hardly believe her eyes when she saw me. She had been walking the floor and praying God [help] me. Florence, about 4 years old, would go away into the bedroom and pray, and come back and say 'Never mind Mama, Poppa will come home alright'"[37]

On another occasion, Haley was instrumental in calling out the men of the community to search for two children who had disappeared in a storm on their way home from school. Haley was the searcher who came upon the frozen corpses just a few hundred feet from shelter.[38] He was called upon to perform the funerals for these unfortunate children.

"This out of doors life, with no reading or mental work was beginning to have a bracing effect on me and I began to feel that I ought to get four oxen and go to work in the Spring on the land."[39] Haley went about getting oxen ("I do not think I ever saw a better four"), feed, a cow, chickens, etc. During this time, he also "travelled around and had Missionary meetings. We had a Magic lantern with about 100 views."[40]

> "It was my custom to rise at 2 a.m. and get the oxen, give them a little chop hitch, and [plow] an acre by about 9 a.m. Then I let them go on the prairie while I had my breakfast. Then I dug stones till noon. Then I sharpened my [plow] shares (2 of them every day) with a forge and anvil, then started to find the oxen. Many times they were a mile or two away. Drove

---

37. Ibid., 123.
38. Ibid., 136.
39. Ibid., 125.
40. Ibid., 126.

them home and ploughed another acre from 3 p.m. to 9. We would take a day off, hitch a team of oxen to a stone boat with the wagon seat on it and we would go calling. It was awful slavery, but I continued to improve."[41]

On another occasion, a prairie fire raced across the land, destroying most of his crop. It would appear that he had a decent harvest about one out of every three years. October 22, 1910, their home was made very happy by the birth of a son, Blake. "He was a big boy of eleven pounds. We had no doctor and had not a little concern over the event, but God knew our need and helped us through."[42]

> "During the winter I had been busy trying to get the district organized as a Rural Municipality as we had no council and nothing was being done on the roads. I succeeded in this and was appointed as the Returning Officer...and got $40.00 for each election. I got $25.00 per year and 2½% of the taxes collected... so these items helped some in those days when money was so scarce."[43]
>
> "I preached at Norfolk school all the summer of 1912 but in harvest some got too busy and finally the congregation got down to nothing so we quit. We had no services that winter and the next spring they wanted me to try again which I did preaching every Sunday till I left the country. They gave me for the first year $22.00 and nothing for the second year."[44]

---

41. Ibid., 128.
42. Ibid., 130.
43. Ibid., 139.
44. Ibid., 142.

Summing up his Saskatchewan experiences, Haley writes,

> "Clearly traceable are the providences of God providing for us temporally in paths of peace. The toils were many, hardships severe and could we have known before what we would have to face we would never have undertaken it, but now that it is past I thank God for it. It has made me a broader man, increased my faith, given me property enough… I have recovered my health and strength which it appears to me I never could have done in any other way. So it appears God led me through it all and brought me out better financially, better in health and better spiritually. To His great Name be all the praise."[45]

> "I was feeling off and on that we had been in secular work long enough. Naturally we thought of going to Africa. This feeling was increased by some losses we had. Heretofore everything had worked together for us… a great prairie fire broke out west of us… our fire [break] got away from us and ran two miles burning [other people's] property to the extent of $600.00. I went around and took a list of what they lost and their valuation, and I paid for it all as soon as I could… Lightning struck two colts I had worth about $450.00… This being an act of God made us feel like leaving the place."[46]

Accordingly, [they] "left for Welland, Ontario where my wife's people live, via Chicago where we attended the Missionary Board meeting. They appointed us to go to Africa in time for the S.A. Mission Conference at Easter 1914. I held

---

45. Ibid., 121.
46. Ibid., 146.

the quarterly meeting at Niagara Falls for Bro. D.E. Allan and they asked us to move there and be their pastor... I took the work over Feb. 6. [1914]"[47]

Haley family with Dorothy, Blake and Florence, ca. 1916

While serving in Niagara Falls, Haley bought a parsonage, paying a substantial amount of the cost from his own savings. Dorothy, ["a good natured little darling"[48]] was born in Welland, August 24, 1914. Finding that his mother was ailing, in September 1915, the Haleys moved to Sarnia to care for the senior Mrs Haley. "It was an honour to be entrusted by God with the care of my old, and now not accountable, Mother, whom He had promised never to leave nor forsake."[49] The several pages that Haley wrote in his *Journal* about the needed care for his mother reflect the pages written when he had heard earlier of the death of his father. Separation from loved ones seemed to bear heavy on him.[50] Remaining in Ontario also allowed them to visit from time to time with Jennie's "home folks" in Welland and superintend the care of John's sister Jennie at Gerry Homes in Gerry, N. Y. While in Sarnia, Haley preached in the churches of several denominations – "fill[ing] a Baptist pulpit in Port Huron and supply[ing] the Methodist churches a

---

47. Ibid., 149.
48. Ibid., 151.
49. Ibid., 153.
50. Ibid., 152-158.

number of times, preaching in the Central Methodist Church the last Sunday I was in Sarnia."[51] He adds the rather interesting comment that [he] "preached a lot of times in our church in Sarnia and received many warm compliments, and some hard knocks."[52] He does not explain the latter comment.

Africa Regained

But still, the undying passion for Africa consumed Haley. So, February 25, 1917, they set sail arriving on March 23rd in Durban, South Africa. As there were difficulties on the Prairies, so they existed on the mission field.

Those years in Mozambique and South Africa were years of many challenges. There was the need to refresh his knowledge of the languages spoken by the nationals.[53] Travel was difficult but necessary – often on foot at great distances; sometimes augmented with the aid of donkeys. Buildings needed to be built, repaired, purchased or sold. Negotiations with government officials required travel and completion of a myriad of forms, but Haley usually managed these well. There was a constant problem with alcoholism among the nationals, and leaders who practiced polygamy and other forms of immorality. It was even necessary to deal with immorality with at least one national pastor. Unfortunately, there were squabbles among the missionaries that Haley had to deal with as District Elder and President of the conference.[54] This made for misunderstanding by other missionaries. This even spread to his own brother Albert and Matilda, his wife, to the extent that they would not

---

51. Ibid., 160.
52. Ibid.
53. Ibid., 237.
54. Ibid., 288, 292.

communicate with JW for some time.[55] But, "by far the greatest event in our home was the birth of Gertrude Mary Peace on July 7th, 1919."[56] Probably equally important was the salvation of Dorothy. "On Dorothy's 9th birthday, I asked her if she would not like it to be her second-birthday. She did not understand, so I explained and she prayed and wept and gave herself to Jesus."[57]

Jennie suffered the "calamity of a miscarriage in December [1917], and for six weeks she was very ill."[58] There was much ongoing concern about their children – sometimes they were in the care of others. Both Florence and Dorothy seemed to have recurring illnesses. They found that costs for schooling were putting them behind, no matter what savings they employed.[59] (Once Florence and Blake were older, there was concern about unhealthy influences by others, as Blake was employed away from home, and Florence was in Nurses' Training in Buffalo, NY. Haley felt that he had "prayed through" for Blake, and that Blake would soon join him in his mission.)

Add to this that, in 1922, now stationed in Benoni, they were in the centre of the Rand Rebellion – surrounded by street fighting and bombing of the city by government forces.

---

55. Ibid., 310.
56. Ibid., 197.
57. Ibid., 209.
58. Ibid., 166.
59. Ibid., 172.

Haley family with Dorothy, Blake, Florence and Peace, ca. 1921

Haley suffered a vitriolic attack by the Missionary Secretary when he misunderstood Haley's position on a matter being discussed in conference.⁶⁰ Fortunately, the secretary realised his error and apologized to Haley the next day. In spite of all those challenges and difficulties, the Haleys pressed on, and he records rapid development, with God able to bring many to salvation in those years in South Africa.⁶¹

It is instructive to record Haley's testimony during these years of his life. "The Lord has given us victory continually, bless His Name. His blood cleanses me from all sin. We make many mistakes but my motives are pure. I am trying to take an hour for prayer each day but many times I do not do it, for which I am greatly poorer. If I do I find clearness of vision and sweet communion and perfect victory."⁶²

---

60. Ibid., 273-274.
61. Ibid., 237, 243; *Life in Mozambique and South Africa*, 88.
62. *Journal*, 263.

The Burning Passion

There was one great passion that kept burning in Haley's soul. That was Central Africa. This can best be told by references to the recurring entries in his *Journal*. As early as December 1922, he writes "I have always had a great drawing towards the Sudan or Central Africa and it seems now that perhaps the Lord would use us to open up a new and needy field, where the need is great and no missionary. I am praying about it, and have written the Missionary Secretary."[63] He wrote a Mr Hurlburt and a Mr Burton, a Pentecostal missionary in the Congo about open fields there. "I put the matter before our board and asked for an amount to be set aside to provide for a preliminary journey to locate a place in Central Africa or the Sudan.[64] He made an appointment with the Consul General of Belgium to discuss the possibility of opening a field in Central Africa. At the end of this appointment, having had considerable discussion, including looking over a map of existing and possible fields, Haley concludes, "So far everything looks favourable."[65] A flurry of letters to officials and missionaries in the Congo follows with the hope that needed information would be available by conference time. "I believe that the Lord is leading in this matter and is calling our church to a needy field and a greater work than we have done."[66]

For several weeks Haley was engaged in working out a compromise between other missionaries and the Missionary Secretary, and a lengthy trip to Inhambane and East African missions, but by May 28, 1924, he approached the Missionary Secretary for permission to scout out the Congo area. "He

63. Ibid., 210.
64. Ibid., 215.
65. Ibid., 216.
66. Ibid., 219.

said I might go up in July if I think best after seeing the Education Commission in July. He says the church wanted just such a field."[67] Realizing that he would need to have facility in the French language, the language of officials in the Belgian Congo, Haley signed up for lessons in the university. All of this, he bathed in prayer, "I do not want to fail the Lord by negligence to pray about it. If anything is done it must be conceived, brought forth and nourished in prayer, 'The wisdom of the world worketh death'. God must be first last and always in the matter."[68] Many cutbacks occurred in the South African field. Haley says that he "anticipate[s] a hard job, salvage operations."[69]

Disheartening news was cabled from the Missionary Secretary in November, 1924; "Financial conditions compelled postponement Sudan project."[70] Haley's response was, "As to the Sudan project, it will come out right. I believe God is in it and will open the way."[71] Time and time again, Haley restated his belief that God would open the way north, in spite of difficulties such as the shortage of funds. He wrote to some friends asking if they would be able to give enough to begin a new work. Some of the other missionaries supported the plan; others were unsure of it. Haley was convinced in his own mind that this was the Lord's will, but thought that a "token" would convince others that this was the way that the mission was to go.[72]

Again, he writes,

"While waiting on God this morning I was drawn

67. Ibid., 252.
68. Ibid., 276.
69. Ibid., 286.
70. Ibid., 277.
71. Ibid., 278.
72. Ibid., 302.

out in prayer that God would take the control of the project for a new field, set the time of departure, lead the way, choose the field, prepare for my family... and give me a special setting of grace, wisdom, and strength of body, soul and spirit, as well as to supply the money and equipment for the journey. The Lord was very near and precious. After prayer my eyes fell on the box of promises on the writing desk and I drew one, thinking I could not always expect to draw appropriate texts, when to my surprise, I got Ps. 32:8. 'I will instruct thee and teach thee in the way that thou shalt go.' Wonderful!...'the way that thou shalt go.' Surely God means to open the way for this trip this year."[73]

A few days later, he and Jennie heard Mrs Studd of the Heart of Africa Mission speak about the Belgian Congo. He found a Christian optician in Johannesburg who told him of his son's missionary work in Kenya. All of these things burned the desire deeper in his heart.

So he began putting things together for an exploratory trip north.[74] He and Jennie talked about Jennie also seeing "the land and the people where she is to work."[75] Again, he claimed the promises of God - "'All power is given unto me in heaven and in earth; go ye therefore.' How wonderful! That answers the question of money...it also speaks of permission to go and all the details of the journey; opening doors with Government officials...My heart rests in this promise..."[76] In an education report, Haley read of disbanded Protestant

---

73. Ibid., 303.
74. Ibid., 300.
75. Ibid., 301.
76. Ibid., 316.

mission stations in Ruanda-Urundi[77] that the Belgian Mandate was trying to re-open.[78]

Furlough

Monday, March 29, 1926 the Haley family boarded ship at Durban for the trip home to Canada.[79] On board ship, he had meetings with people knowledgeable about missions in Central Africa, and continued strategizing ways and means of getting there to evaluate the situation.[80] Making connections for Canada in London, England, he had time to meet with a representative of the British and Foreign Missionary Society who told him that Urundi was "absolutely untouched by Protestant missions." Heartened by this, Haley concludes that, as "[God] has been calling us He must also have been calling the church to prayer and action along these lines."[81] At Chicago, for meetings of the Missions Board, Haley spoke briefly at the meeting of the Woman's Missionary Society and the board itself. It looked like things would begin to happen. While in Canada, he continued to work on the project, even suggesting that the Canadian church take over the project of a new field: he felt that the answer was on the way.

Given the amount of time and effort that Haley was spending in writing to and meeting with government officials and other missionaries, one might conclude that he was not continuing his day-to-day work. Such was not the case. He

---

77. References made to Urundi may be confusing to the reader. This was the name of this Belgian Mandate until it was separated from Ruanda and became an independent state – Burundi – its present name, July 1, 1962. For purposes of uniformity and faithfulness to the time of Haley's work there, this chapter retains the original name.
78. Ibid., 332.
79. Ibid., 369.
80. Ibid., 373, 378-380, 382.
81. Ibid., 402, 403.

wrote the draft of *Life in Mozambique and South Africa*, as well as making necessary preparations for furlough in Canada.[82] Furlough, when it came, allowed him to travel from Ontario to New York and Pennsylvania, to Virginia and Alabama, to Washington DC, Michigan and to drive to Saskatchewan and Alberta. Everywhere he went, he spread the missionary challenge.

Haley held many revival services, and loved getting involved with the altar services. At one of these, where somehow he 'got in charge of the altar service', [it would appear that he had exhorted the gathering to come forward] while listening to testimonies that seemed to go on and on, the District Elder came to him and said, "You got this thing going, you will have to get it stopped."[83] (This revival –altar service experience would well serve him and the Protestant missions in Central Africa in later years. An Anglican missionary confessed to him that they would not have known what to do in revival services, had it not been for learning from Haley's previous experience.) But all was not seriousness for Haley: at another service in Pennsylvania, he reported that the preacher was doing very well until one of his garters let loose.[84] He tobogganed with President Garlock at Chili Seminary, near Rochester, NY – he confessed that both were the worse for the wear - so they left it to the students.[85] He made arrangements for Blake to stay at Chili and continue school, and for Florence to enter nurses' training in Buffalo.[86] Toward the end of their furlough they spent three weeks at the lakeside cottage of Rev C. V. Fairbairn,[87] who would later become the first Canadian to serve as a bishop in the Free

82. Ibid., 347.
83. Ibid., 446.
84. Ibid., 438.
85. Ibid., 450.
86. Ibid., 472, 475.

Methodist Church. Back in South Africa, he reported that they had travelled a total of 42,000 miles from start to finish on this furlough.[88]

But then, bad news - the board decided that they could not move forward. "It seemed so strange to me after they had supported it for ten years and in 1926 voted unanimously to open one. I cannot feel they have done the will of God...I am yet believing they will reverse their decision."[89] At Christmas, 1930, the Mission Secretary, in response to further inquiries from Haley, said the board thought it would be wise for Haley to send a memorial to General Conference. Taking it up with the World Dominion Movement, Haley was informed that, "Urundi is still open and would be a suitable field with plenty of scope for a mission."[90] Monday, April 6, 1931 Haley received the following cablegram, "'Directors permit immediate trip Central Africa if financed from farm and hut rent funds. Letter follows,' signed, Olmstead."[91]

On March 20, 1932, Haley received official permission "from the Minister for Colonies in Brussels to establish our work in Ruanda-Urundi."[92] He records it as a "notable day."

So, May 31, 1932, Haley, his son Blake and fellow missionary Frank Adamson headed north in a trip to scout out the land. Getting to the border of Northern Rhodesia and the Congo, they found that they would need to abandon the car, so Blake and Adamson turned back, and Haley went on alone. By train and steamer on Lake Tanganyika, he arrived at Usumbura, where he was met by a Danish Baptist Missionary,

---

87. Ibid., 478, 479. Haley wrote "It was so nice. We bathed and fished – caught fish – lots of them...I longed for a summer home there."
88. Ibid., 481.
89. Ibid., 494.
90. Ibid., 501.
91. Ibid., 501.
92. Ibid., 530.

"Brother Jensen." (Interestingly, we never find this man's first name in Haley's *Journal*: he is always simply a valued brother.) This man, after testing Haley's orthodoxy, especially regarding the authenticity of the Scriptures, became "joined at once in the most cordial bond of fellowship."[93] A true brother from then onward, Jensen boarded Haley at the Baptist Mission station and eventually the Haley family for a time; served as their taxi until Haley could get his own vehicle, received and forwarded his mail, translated for Haley in discussions with officials, and helped him complete required documents in French. Two more years were to pass before the way opened for the family to move northward.

Moving Northward at Last

Now, the memory of the scouting trip burning within him, Haley concluded that the Rubicon had been crossed, and it was time for action. "By 1934 we had completed our seven years' term in South Africa, and were due for furlough. But my heart was in Urundi, and furlough made no appeal. I represented to the home authorities that as we were five it would cost a considerable amount of money to take us home, and bring us back, but if they gave us permission to open a new field and gave us the allowances we were then receiving, we would trust the Lord for all our needs for travel to the land 3,000 miles away, for opening the work, house building, and other things as they came along. Even at this they could not escape responsibility in some greater degree, so when the debt and depression-burdened Missionary Secretary said, 'Loose him and let him go.' It was no inconsiderable act of faith. On the other hand an African missionary on furlough, attending the meeting, counselled, 'You may as well let him go, for he will go anyway.'"[94]

---

93. Haley, *But Thy Right Hand*, 17.

Jennie "did not look forward with pleasure to breaking up our home, leaving our people, the flowers, the sea, and all the lovely memories …as the children grew up, to begin again in the wilds. We had pioneered from the beginning. Why not let younger people do it now? …The reason was that God had called us… If I was going she wanted to go… the money the Lord had given was only sufficient for one. Her distress was painful and touching… I asked her what I should do, and she being entirely cast upon the Lord, even as I was, said through her tears, 'You will have to go,' and she took it to the Lord in prayer."[95]

About the same time that Haley was setting forth into Central Africa to find inner peace for the call that God had placed upon him, a young theologian, Deitrich Bonhoeffer, speaking at a conference in Germany made a statement that Haley would have endorsed gladly: "Peace means giving oneself completely to God's commandment, wanting no security, but in faith and obedience laying the destiny of the nations in the hand of Almighty God, not trying to direct it for selfish purposes. Battles are won, not with weapons, but with God. They are won when the way leads to the cross."[96]

Finding that surety deposits would be required by each person in his family, he continued to have faith that God would eventually "open up the way for all members of the family." A Methodist Episcopal missionary in the Congo offered to come and introduce Haley to the Governor. Haley began in earnest to publicize his plans with brochures sent to the home churches, and to get matters sorted out with government officials to cover required monetary guarantees. Finally, he was able to cable the Missionary Secretary, "My deposit made. Sailing November."[97] Eventually, after Haley

---

94. Ibid., 24.
95. Ibid., 27.
96. Eric Metaxas, *Bonhoeffer*, New York: Nelson Publishing, 241.

spoke with the Governor, the need for all deposits was dropped, the deposit that Haley had made for himself was returned, and the mission was recognized and approved to apply for a site.[98] The way opened up for Haley to take over Muyebe, as site mandated to the Danish Baptist Mission that they were unable to service. Additionally, government officials gave him permission to seek out another site sanctioned by the government.

Moving Prayerfully into Urundi

Money was in short supply in the North American church, but, fortunately, Haley had some individuals who remembered his need and provided support above and beyond the family's support from the mission[99] - it all seemed to come, miraculously, just when he was beginning to run out of funds. So, being housed by Jensen and the Danish Mission, while waiting for final government approval to enter Urundi, Haley started making door and window frames[100] for the house that he would build. He kept working on his study of French (French being spoken in the home in Musema where he stayed with other missionaries), and took up Kirundi as a third language.[101] He also drew up plans for the buildings to be erected and the grounds of the new site at Muyebe. March 22, the 30th wedding anniversary of his marriage to Jennie, passed quietly.[102]

---

97. Haley, *Journal*, 578.
98. Ibid., 592, 593.
99. Ibid., 548.
100. Ibid., 604.
101. Ibid., 594.
102. Ibid., 621.

A local chief in Burundi

Jensen accompanied Haley on March 1, 1935 when they went to meet the Big Chief, who readily gave them permission to choose a site for the mission. This they did the following day, -- the date of this all-important beginning was May 2, 1935 -- marking a site at Muyebe that had a steady stream of water flowing from a natural spring. Haley had received word that this former German station at Muyebe had been turned over to the Danish Mission, which in turn was willing to let Haley occupy it. Jensen helped in setting up the tent and getting the local people to bring building materials, and providing workers from his area. Other materials that Haley had previously ordered had also arrived on the site. With these they constructed a grass kitchen, sanitary arrangements, and a workshop 12 x 18 feet.

Note the wisdom of the man in this early encounter with the people of the area. Haley spoke to local natives who were sitting nearby watching all of this, explaining that he had come to live among them and that he was ready to start a school for them when they wanted to learn. "They should tell us and we would all stop a day and build a little grass school. My houses are mine and I pay for them. The school is theirs. I will not eat or sleep in it. They must build it. They readily agreed. This is the beginning of self support or the mission doing the things they ought to do, so it is vital."[103]

This marked a change in the way in which Haley would now do missions. He began with prayer at the door of his tent the next morning, being observed in all of his actions by natives of the area. Haley's experience in South Africa had been in fairly traditional missionary work - in which the sending country supplied the missionary and the funds to build up the mission, and even to use donated funds to reward native pastor-teachers for their work in spreading the Gospel to other points. Unfortunately, this practice tended to set these pastor-teachers apart from their peers, as they were considered to be more wealthy than others. Haley had observed that this set up a barrier that prevented the spread of the Gospel.

Haley's early camp at Muyebe

Just twelve days after Haley's arrival, along with the men who came to work, twelve little boys came to be taught. "They were only half clad in bark and not clean, but it is a good

103. Ibid., 636.

beginning and will grow. Then during the day one of the workmen said to me that he wanted to learn, so after work at 3:30 pm we had about 20 minutes for them, six in all, I believe. Praise the Lord! He makes great oaks from small acorns and may our church be used to bring thousands and hundreds of thousands of the Burundi to Christ."[104] Perhaps this is why a later author (Bates) called him a prophet. Looking ahead, he wrote to the Mission Board and requested that the Adamson family be assigned to Kayero, the other mission site that he had previously marked out.

In spite of the fact that Roman Catholics were attempting to prevent children from coming to the school, Haley went ahead assisting the natives to build a little school. After all had worked for him during the day, they then, voluntarily, went to building the school building with materials that they had brought. "I gave the poles and cords and reeds and bamboos, or most of them, but the principle established, that it is their work and I am only helping them is the main thing."[105] (A full description of how the schooling operated is found on pages 51 to 56 of *But Thy Right Hand*.) The first church service was held in it the following Sunday, and morning prayer each weekday. This marked three years since Haley, Blake and Adamson had left South Africa to scout out the land.[106]

Making bricks and tiles, marking out roadways and flower and garden beds (to help Jennie acclimatize to the place?), building a garage/office building, and purchasing building materials brought by the natives consumed much of Haley's days. Still he found time for his daily devotions, to do his correspondence, and prepare a monthly newsletter, all the while teaching school to 20 to 40 children, and masonry

104. Ibid., 647.
105. Ibid., 654.
106. Ibid., 655.

skills to others. As noted earlier, he continued to make his door and window frames from rough sawn lumber that had to be planed by hand. He decided that it was best to hire only local men, and so sent home to other areas those who had helped in starting the work. All were paid out of the funds that friends continued to provide – these arriving *by chance* just as his funds were running out. One such gift was enough that he could send it to Jennie to pay their ways northward.[107]

Jennie, Dorothy, J W and Peace Haley in Burundi

Jennie, Dorothy and Peace arrived July 16, 1935, with the assistance of Brother Jensen, to the challenges of what was dubiously called the White House. "The walls, plaster and floors were wet. Calico served for glass and boxes and scrap lumber for doors, where there were any. Grass grew up in the mud floor until my wife had it dug up like a plowed field in an effort to get it dry. We all had colds, and to relieve the

---

107. Ibid., 658.

distress fires were made in old gasoline tins, which with the smoke reduced everyone to tears."[108] Within a few weeks, Haley had made a cook stove out of bricks, with a paraffin tin for an oven, as well as board doors for the windows and doors of the house. In January 1936, he began to build their permanent house, making bricks and roof tiles in a kiln that he had constructed.[109] Very shortly after their arrival, Peace took over the work in the dispensary, giving 50 to 75 treatments every day, and Dorothy took over the office work, being designated the legal representative for those times when Haley might be away from the mission.[110]

The White House, first home of Haley's family in Burundi

Just four months after arriving on the field, Haley held his

---

108. *But Thy Right Hand*, 40.
109. *Journal*, 677.
110. Ibid., 670.

first service in his new Kirundi language. Over fifty natives were there, "The Lord was there and I'm sure He spoke to hearts."[111] A month later, Haley, "felt it was time to take an expression as to who wanted to go with us for I felt that there were a number who had in their own minds definitely cast in their lot with us. Accordingly I asked [those] who wanted to follow Jesus to stand. A group of young men rose, and then the whole congregation of over fifty. We felt God was in it and prayed earnestly for them. The next Sunday, Sept. 29th, I asked those who wanted to pray for Jesus to take away their bad hearts to stand and a number rose. Then we had each pray for himself. It was perhaps the first time they had ever prayed to Jesus."[112] Six men came in the evening in response to Haley's invitation. As a follow-up, he instituted a "seekers meeting each Sunday afternoon and there are hopeful cases. Praise the Lord!"[113] The Haleys also attended a conference of missionaries that included the Belgian Protestant Society, The Church Missionary Society (Anglican), Danish Baptists, and The Friends Africa Gospel Mission. This attitude of cooperation with like-minded groups was to be a hallmark of his mission work.

"Self support" was central to Haley's concept of missions. It was crucial to determine how and when this should be instituted. "We knew from past experience how difficult it is to bring a church to self-support whose pastors have been paid by the Mission, for the pastors, who are leaders of their people, are usually opposed to the change, for obvious reasons, and the people, on whom the change imposes financial responsibility to which they are not accustomed, are naturally reluctant to undertake it."[114]

111. Ibid., 672.
112. Ibid., 678.
113. Ibid., 686.
114. *But Thy Right Hand*, 56

The people of the area had little money, so leaders should not expect great amounts either. When all of this was explained to the people, they assented to the plan, and established the hoped-for amount that each person would bring to provide payment for pastor-teachers going to outposts that were springing up everywhere. These offerings were voluntary and did not limit the attendance of anyone at school.[115] In order to teach church government, it was announced, "that a locked iron box with two keys would be bought. The keys would be given to two members of the group, one a pastor-teacher and one a layman. The box would be kept in the home of the missionary. It would be taken to the church by them, and, after the offering, opened in the presence of the congregation. The offering would be deposited in the box, recorded in the book, all would be relocked, and the box would go back to the mission house."[116] Since offerings could include beans, corn, sweet potatoes, eggs wood or anything else that the natives had, bushel baskets were used for the offerings. These were then sold at fair market value or retained until the market price increased. The accounts were audited annually.[117]

---

115. Ibid., 57.
116. Ibid., 59.
117. Ibid., 60, 61. The reader is encouraged to read the full account of this ingenious method of providing for the needs of local churches, congregations and their leaders.

Dorothy Haley with her father and school children

In spite of trouble from the Roman Catholics – beatings of children, and spies reporting them to the priests – the schools continued to grow. At Muyebe attendance soared to three and four hundred. Students came with raw banana leaves on which they wrote with a grass stem. In support of the native pastor-teachers, Dorothy would ride a motorcycle to outpost schools. The students would be there to greet her, "rush for the school, a few hymns and choruses she had taught them, silence during prayer, recitation in unison of the Apostles' Creed, the Lord's Prayer, the story of creation, certain chapters from the Gospels, some reading, and in half an hour, after a closing prayer, all accompanied her for a distance, some rushing ahead and some following, all in the height of good fellowship. All along the way, they dropped out with their 'Nakasaka,[118]' a parting greeting, some having

---

118. alternatively, and probably more properly "N'agasaga"

followed a mile or two."[119] With the growth of these outpost schools, pressure on the Muyebe school abated, and it was possible to provide training for teachers. This became the embryo of a Bible and [teacher-training] Normal School. The number of students in schools had risen to over one thousand.[120]

Peace Haley with Burundian friends

Peace continued her work in the dispensing of medicines in the open. Since so many would crowd around her, a little grass shelter six feet square was built, with a door at each end. The patients could then pass through one at a time and receive her ministrations. Peace planted flowers and morning glories beside it, and it soon became known as the Morning Glory Clinic. All kinds of ailments were presented; patients came from as far away as twenty miles. A gift of $500.00 was received, which allowed for a brick building, where mothers and children could be out of the sun and rain as they waited

119. Ibid., 62, 63.
120. Ibid., 63

for treatment. Following the "self-support" principle, patients were charged a small fee, but none were turned away for lack of funds. Several native dispensers were trained, one specializing in pulling teeth. "The Barundi way of extracting [teeth had been] to flatten a four inch nail and pry out the offending tooth while several friends sat on the patient."[121] A simple service was held each morning, "thus reaching with the gospel [up to] four hundred persons per day."[122] Eventually, and before the government had set up a hospital about four miles away, Miss Marjorie Peach and Miss Margaret Holton, both Registered Nurses who had studied tropical diseases in Belgium, came to Muyebe to assist in this all-important work.

Jennie, often in the background, as was her wish, became "Mother" to all. She gathered slips, roots, bulbs and seeds from far and wide. "Vegetables we had in abundance, and the strawberry season lasted nine months. Red raspberries and black were bearing; oranges, lemons, and peaches had been planted, and even an apple tree and two grapevines had been raised from seeds. Already 'Mother' was supplying the new missions we opened with cuttings, roots and seeds as well as fruit for jam and vegetables for those who began on virgin soil."[123] Haley reports that on one occasion Jennie entertained eight government officials plus the four of them in their 12 x 12 dining room in the White House. Guests often came unannounced, but Jennie cared for all.[124]

Supported by native offerings, two converts began teaching basic charts, Bible stories and hymns in village schools. Haley sent two more to Kayero, since there was no house there yet in which he could live. "Pastor Matayo Myiruko, Haley's servant as a boy, taught to read and write by

---

121. Ibid., 67.
122. Ibid.
123. Ibid., 70.
124. Ibid.

him and promoted to catechist/teacher (later to become pastor and superintendent), tells this story: One time we came back to Bgana [Mister] Haley discouraged and determined to give up our work as village teachers. I and some others brought our attendance notebooks and presented them to Bgana Haley. 'We are quitting,' we said. 'The work is too hard.' Haley did not protest or argue but accepted the notebooks and said, 'All right, but before you go let's pray together.' We all got down on our knees and Haley prayed. I asked Pastor Matayo what happened next. He said shyly, 'We picked up our notebooks and went back to work.'"[125]

Haley brick home in Muyebe

Progress on the Muyebe house was slow, since some workers lacked skills, and finally Haley took over the finishing work himself. It wasn't until February, 1937 that they were able to occupy part of the new house. Haley reports, "We are now quite comfortable and home seems so nice. I think we are

---

125. Bates, "Prophet and Apostle," *Free Methodist Historical Society Newsletter*, Summer 2001, 1.

about ready now for new missionaries. I want to go to Kayero next week and have the men hew stones for a building...I have written the Miss. Sec'y to send the Adamsons direct to Urundi in July."[126] Miss Esther Shelhammer, along with her parents, who came to get her settled, joined as a new recruit for the mission. "On May 7th, 1938, the Colletts and Miss Gonsolus arrived. The Colletts were "over and above" what the Board [had] expected to send and were a direct answer to prayer.[127] Along with the visiting Missionary Secretary, Haley marked out and applied for a site at Kibuye, and settled the Colletts at Kayero. Haley returned two weeks later, with native help, to build a house there at Kayero. By the end of 1938, there were four mission sites approved. August 26, 1936, Haley wrote, "I have attained unto 58 years, in the mercy of the Lord. Why he has spared so unprofitable a servant I do not know, but He becomes sweeter as the days go by and there is now no thought of resisting His will. It is the only good. Praise His Name!"[128]

As the pages of Haley's *Journal* start to run out, there is a sense that he is beginning to realize that he will need to begin 'handing off' to others. Hospitalization for a time, because of a recurring bout of malaria, was a complicating factor. In his *Journal*, there is record of the almost frenetic activities designed to put stations and people in place, the references to new missionaries as noted above, and passing references to other developments that are taking place. Then come the poignant words, "but must get away and have a rest, after 10½ years to get ready for it all."[129] Ironically,

---

126. *Journal*, 734.
127. The Mission Board had refused to send the Colletts to Africa, due to a shortness of funds. Their acceptance by another mission caused the harvest-deprived farmers of Saskatchewan to raise additional funds to send them off, bringing fruition to Haley's prayer for workers.
128. Ibid., 721.

but perhaps an indication of great fatigue, the last paragraph of his *Journal* records that he has taken Brother Collett to Matana for treatment for Tick Fever on February 26. The last line says that Collett is still there February 5 (a confusion of dates?) It was time for a rest, after ten and a half very demanding years without furlough.[130]

New Responsibilities

Things did begin to change on Haleys' return to Urundi in April, 1940. John Wesley and Jennie were joined by Dorothy and her husband Burton McCready, and Peace and her husband Oddvar Berg.[131] The Colletts were at Kibuye, and Adamsons, Ila Gonsolus and Esther Shelhammer were at Muyebe. Nurses Marjory Peach and Margaret Holton came shortly thereafter. Haley exulted, "How the work has grown! In December 1934, 'with my staff, I crossed over this Jordan,' and now we have Muyebe, Kayero, Kibuye and Rwintare all occupied by missionaries and recently the Administrator called me to accompany him to the mission site applied for last year, Myeya.[132]

---

129. Ibid., 744.
130. Ibid.
131. Oddvar was the jokester in the family. The occasion when he stuffed his Uncle Albert's pockets at a family gathering with silverware, and then "accused" him, as he was leaving, of trying to steal these valuables, became an oft-repeated tale.
132. *Congo-Nile Notes*, July, 1940.

Free Methodist Church at Muyebe

But, Haley kept looking northward. Less than a year later, he wrote, "How great is the door that is opened to us I have no idea, but before I went on furlough in 1938 I looked over a new area 150 miles from here and I have not been able to forget that group of people since. We talked to the Lord about it and He sent us a gift of nearly $1,000.00 that could be used at our discretion... Accordingly, a party of four set out."[133] Even though war was raging in Europe, funds were in short supply, new recruits prevented by war, and the Italian army was threatening to come south, he applied for and was granted a site at Kibogora, a heavily populated area where, characteristically he concluded, that a hospital should be built there as well. Shortly thereafter, he was making plans and was granted a site for a rest camp for missionaries of all evangelical missions engaged in Central Africa.[134]

133. Ibid., May 1941.

Revival, which started among Haley's Anglican friends was racing through the country. At a large convention in September 1942 at Muyebe, Haley tells of "heart searching and seeking after purity of heart" among the three thousand Africans and sixty-three missionaries with their families. The president of the Alliance wrote to Haley, "…the Lord did great things for us, which humanly speaking might never have happened but for the wider appreciation of revival which your experience gave us. So with all our hearts we thank you and praise the Lord."[135]

That role of spiritual leader became more and more the call of God for Haley. He wrote, preached, planned, counselled and prayed. "A missionary doctor of the Church Missionary Society referred to him later as that 'grand old veteran and missionary statesman.'"[136]

One further development in Haley's approach to missions followed. Calls were coming in from distant areas, but missionaries were already spread thin. "A number of African leaders, along with Haley and some of the missionaries met together to decide how to respond. They sat in a small circle; no one had much to say; finally there was just silence. Haley led out in prayer and then others followed, quietly, one by one. After a rather long time of prayer the following resolution was drafted: 'The feeling is strong upon us that God is calling the Barundi church to go forward with the Gospel to those areas where it has not yet come. And being convinced that the coming of the Lord draweth nigh, we the representatives of the Barundi Church assembled at Kibuye, recommend that we proceed at once to occupy new areas as follows…'"[137] The infant church accepted the call of

---

134. Bates, *Soul Afire*, 55.
135. *The Missionary Tidings,* September 1942, 263.
136. Op. cit., 65.
137. Ibid., 67.

ten young men to go, and agreed to accept responsibility for their support. "Money is coming in and bands are going out, sent by the Church, to hold special meetings everywhere at our older points. Hundreds are coming to the Lord here in the home area and we are waiting to have the reports of these men going out [to the distant assignments.]"[138]

Furlough

The Haleys left Africa in October 1946 for another furlough. Missionaries and nationals alike were sad to see them go; the nationals prayed earnestly for their safety: "Please God be the driver of the big machine [aeroplane] that takes our Bgana Mukuru [Great Master] and Madamu Mukuru [Great Mistress] to the foreign land, because it [the machine] has no wisdom, and Lord help them to tell the people over there of the great need here for workers, and give them a good rest and bring them back to us soon."[139]

Tirelessly travelling, speaking, writing and teaching, John Wesley Haley and his wife Esther Jane (Jennie) came to the end of their days, he on January 6, 1951 and she on April 29, 1952, in Cleveland, Ohio. They are buried in Lakeview Cemetery, Welland, Ontario.

The choice of St Luke's description of Barnabas for John Wesley Haley's funeral service, Rev G. W. Stevens officiating, was a most appropriate one – "For he was a good man, full of the Holy Spirit and of faith, and much people was added unto the Lord" (Acts 11:24).

Gerald Bates, recounts a meeting of African leaders, in which Free Methodist work was reviewed, with special emphasis on the work of Haley. Older native pastors spoke of Haley and his indomitable vision. "Out of the group, from a

---

138. *Congo-Nile Notes*, December 1946.
139. Ibid.

young man, came the question, 'Had Haley no faults?' 'Oh, I suppose so,' Pastor Matayo replied, 'I am sure he was human. But, let me tell you, there has never been another like him.'"[140]

Burton Hamilton -- Author's Note

When approached by John McCready about the idea of writing this biographical section of a work to explain the methodology of John Wesley Haley, I immediately questioned my right or ability to attempt such a task. The possibility of other writers was explored, but the pendulum came swinging back to me.

Having some faint childhood memories of John Wesley Haley visiting in our home, I felt, and still feel my inadequacy to this task. Such was the measure of the man in my family and church circles that I feared that I could not rise to the occasion.

But, here now is my effort. The reader will note that I have spent a considerable amount of time on the religious and social activities and communities into which John Wesley Haley came. I have tried to prise out as much as possible about this, because I feel that it had a great deal of influence on his development and later life. Unfortunately, and perhaps this is an indication of the humility and meekness of the man, there is very little to be found about his early life.

School records are nonexistent*, and there is a period of the "silent years" between 1878 and 1898, except for the incident related to me by my grandfather. Accordingly, I conclude that his early days in the church, his personal relationship with God, his early experiences on the mission field, and his hard days on the Prairies made him into the pioneering giant that he became.

I should further note that I have not recorded a great deal

---

140. Bates, "Prophet," 2.

of detail about the growth of the mission – other parts of this document will illumine that. The reader is referred to *Life in Mozambique and South Africa, But Thy Right Hand,* and *Soul Afire* as well for greater detail about Haley's work in South Africa. I have attempted rather to focus almost entirely on the development of the man himself.

I would also encourage the reader to go to John Wesley Haley's hand written *Journal* that is housed in the Archives of Spring Arbor University. Susan M. Panak and members of her staff have been most helpful in providing access to the *Journal*, and other periodicals, for my use in research for this document. (See Appendix A for a note about the *Journal.*)

When contacting school records officials, we were informed that we would need to have Power of Attorney to access such records, if they did in fact exist. Hardly possible, when even the individual's children are deceased.

2

The Manuscript

John Wesley Haley

> "Moses was admonished of God when he was about
> to make the tabernacle:
> for, See, saith he, *that* thou make all things
> according to the pattern shewed to thee" (Heb 8:5).

FOREWORD

J.W. Haley

Since the attention of missionary movements were called to the study of their systems by Roland Allen's "startling" book, *Missionary Methods, St. Paul's or Ours?* in 1912, various useful contributions have been made to this cause by missionaries from most of the mission fields of the world. Many of these record the eminently successful efforts that have been brought into being; large national churches that have, in a great measure, assumed the responsibility for the evangelization of their people. These outstanding examples are the bright spots on the world horizon, for with the generally conceded statement that "there are more heathen in the world today than there were one hundred years ago," we are confronted with the fact that all methods are not succeeding. To meet this distressing situation, the call is made for more money, more missionaries and more equipment. While all this is good, should we not ask ourselves the question, "will the extra money we may be able to raise be commensurate with the situation and turn our failure into success?" Quite evidently, it will not and the matter must not be dismissed in terms of money, missionaries and equipment. On these terms, the Apostolic Church must have conspicuously failed, but the truth is that it conspicuously succeeded. In our own time, we have seen that mission fields like Madagascar and Ethiopia, being left without missionaries and facing opposition, have doubled their membership to the amazement of missionaries when they were re-admitted.

Have not we been obsessed with the idea of the necessity of foreign control of all spiritual movements and so have eliminated spontaneity? And yet, spontaneity is the very genius of the Gospel. Philip teaches the Queen's Treasurer and the message goes into Ethiopia. Paul preached in Antioch, in Pisidia and, "as many as were ordained to eternal life believed. And the word of the Lord was published throughout all the region" (Acts 13:48-49). Such spontaneous outbreaks have occurred in recent times, but have been suppressed or regularized because, being of little faith, we fear them.

The author of *Missionary Methods*, finds the cause of much of our failure in our methods, which are in such sharp contrast with those of Paul, which succeeded. The purpose of the present brochure is to incite to a study of New Testament order, which order is illustrated by the presence of expanding, spontaneous, churches in many parts of the world. Especially, Board members and executives directing missionary efforts should be informed on methods that fail and methods that succeed.

With the conviction that what I have gleaned during the fifty years since I volunteered for pioneer missionary effort, should be made available to those who are enlisted in the cause, or soon to join the present crusade to make Christ known, I submit these pages, praying God to use them for

His own glory and the salvation of the souls of men. The emancipation of national churches from foreign financial control, would doubtless, in many cases, provide the impetus for spontaneity.

How to produce an indigenous church from groups sustained by foreign money and under foreign control is a question searchingly asked by many missionaries today. The task would have been simpler, from the beginning, but is not impossible, if we are willing with John to "decrease," or with Jesus to be "among you as he that serveth" (Luke 22:27).

The author wishes to acknowledge his indebtedness to The Friendship Press for kind permission to quote from *Madras Series* and *The Church in the New Jamaica* and to A.C. Stanley Smith, M.D. for his article on "Revival" in *Congo Mission News* and to Miss Alice Walls for editing.[1]

CHAPTER I

The Unfinished Task

"Go ye into all the world and preach the Gospel to every creature" (Mark 16:15). Was it impossible?

The unchallenged statement that there are more heathen in the world today than ever before can only be painful to the Church to which came the command of the ascending Saviour as recorded in Matthew.

> And Jesus came and spake unto them, saying, All power is given unto me in heaven and in earth. Go ye therefore, and teach all nations, baptizing them

---

1. Alice Walls (1887-1959), a Bachelor of Arts graduate of the University of Toronto, was the first woman ordained as a Deacon in the Free Methodist Church in Canada (1918), serving as pastor, then teacher and principal of Lorne Park College, as well as editor of *Missionary Tidings*.

in the name of the Father and of the Son, and of the Holy Ghost: Teaching them to observe all things whatsoever I have commanded you: and, lo, I am with you alway, *even* unto the end of the world. Amen (Matt 28:18-20).

The sweeping statements of the commission — all power, teach all nations, baptizing them, teaching them to observe all things, whatsoever I have commanded you, and, I am with you always — seem to look forward to a triumphant movement of the Church, by means of which all nations would soon be taught.

That the Apostles, to whom the commission was given, so understood it, is confirmed by their activities as recorded in the New Testament and in Church history. With the Herculean efforts of St. Paul, the New Testament makes us familiar, but we must also have recourse to records of later origin for the acts of the others. In the early centuries of Christianity, Christian dioceses flourished in North Africa, and Matthew, who probably planted them, penetrated as far south as Ethiopia to end his career. The Coptic Church of that land, which, though it lost much of the simplicity of the Gospel of Christ, during the following centuries, witnesses nevertheless, that the Apostles accepted the command of their Lord as being possible of accomplishment speedily, if not wholly, in their day. Thomas, no longer doubting, found in India, an outlet for his faith and established a Church that is still traceable and active to this day. Thus, before the death of the Apostles, much of Africa, Europe and Asia had been taught.

While our Lord was yet with His disciples, He stressed the lesson of urgency. The kingdom was "at hand" (Matt 4:17), the axe was "laid at the root of the trees" (Matt 3:10). He said "Go" and "As ye go, preach, ... Provide neither gold, nor silver, nor brass in your purses, ... for your journey, neither two coats, neither shoes, nor yet staves" (Matt 10:9-10). The emphasis is on "provide." Do not take time to accumulate things. The matter is urgent. Your needs will be supplied. The seventy were sent with similar urgency. "Carry neither purse nor scrip and salute no man by the way" (Luke 10:4). Go with expedition. The matter is urgent.

It is true that later, after His rejection, and when the King, instead of having been placed on the throne of David was placed on a cross, He said, "But now he that hath a purse let him take *it*, and likewise *his* scrip: and he that hath no sword, let him sell his garment, and buy one" (Luke 22:36), but the urgency of the trust was not removed. Indeed, it is present in His resurrection – ascension command.

When we consider this note of urgency in our Lord's attitude to His business, the reaction of the disciples to His command, and the global results achieved in the few remaining years of their lives, we may well wonder why the task was not accomplished in, at least, a generation, or two. The answer may be found in the declension of the Church with a comparative cessation of extension effort through the "dark ages" and medevial times. "While the bridegroom tarried, they all slumbered and slept. And at midnight there was a cry made, Behold, the bridegroom cometh; go ye out to meet him" (Matt 25:5-6). The midnight cry may well refer to the awakening of the Church in her responsibility to a world without God a century and a half ago. Since then the Church has again addressed herself to the task of world evangelization with great zeal and courage, but with methods that differ essentially from those of the Apostolic Church.

In addressing herself to her task, she has deemed it necessary to thoroughly prepare herself, and has established many and great halls of learning, so that instead of being under the necessity of sending "unlearned and ignorant men," as was our Lord, she has at her call today, the most highly trained workers in the corresponding branches of science. Her servants are not able to say with Peter and John, "Silver and gold have I none," for most of them are well supplied with money and modern conveniences.

If we think of a Matthew pressing forward on foot, by camel or by sailing boat, with a few traveling companions, staying long enough in a place, here and there, to establish a Church, we may well wonder how he found it possible, during the years that remained of his life, to found churches over so wide an area. And when we consider his mobility and the resultant vast accomplishments are we not left with a conviction of frustration over the modern "mission station", an institution unknown in Matthew's time, where we find ourselves anchored for fifty years, and even then, fear that it would fail if left without a foreign shepherd? He left the flock in the care of the Elders, chosen, endued and put in charge by the Holy Spirit. He ordained these God-appointed shepherds and passed on.

It is this comparative paucity of results in many missions, this defeat, if "there are more heathen in the world now than ever before," notwithstanding the great resources in workers and wealth, at the disposition of the Church over these years, when viewed on the background of the fewness of workers and poverty of the early Church with their glorious achievements, that creates a gnawing dissatisfaction in men's hearts. Can we be satisfied with this defeat, this comparative stagnation, notwithstanding that there is this urgency upon us? Does not the situation call for a comprehensive study and an intensive examination of methods with a view to the elimination of fruitless ones? In our study, "to whom shall we go," but to the Head of the Church and to His Word? "All scripture *is* given by inspiration, and *is* profitable for doctrine, for reproof, for correction, for instruction in righteousness:

That the man of God may be perfect, thoroughly furnished unto all good works" (2 Tim 3:16-17).

CHAPTER II

The Church: God's Instrument for World Redemption

It is significant that Jesus would not permit his disciples to do anything towards the founding of the Church until the arrival of the Holy Spirit, "the promise of the Father." This was not alone that they might be prepared by tarrying, important as that was, but the Holy Spirit, who proceedeth from the Father and the Son, is their Executive during the church dispensation and only He could be entrusted with so important a matter as building the body of Christ. In Matthew, He makes the declaration, "I will build my Church" (16:18). Paul and others may be said to have planted churches but Christ Himself is the builder whose blueprints we are to follow. And as Moses was admonished by God to "make all things according to the pattern" (Heb 8:5), so we are not free to disregard His pattern for the Church, which He loved and gave Himself for, which He purchased with His own blood, and of which He is the chief cornerstone, body and head. He is a jealous God and will not give His place as Head of the Church to another.

As He saw it, it was expedient for the Church that He go away, that He send the Comforter, the Holy Spirit (John 16:7) to abide, as guide, and author of the new birth (John 3:5-6), the inspirer of Scripture, and the source of wisdom and power to appoint and send ministers (Acts 13:2-4), and to direct where they shall preach. That He retains this office in the Church is evident inasmuch as He still calls men to preach, and even an apostle could not choose his own field (Acts 16:6-10).

Immediately after His arrival, accompanied by "a sound

from heaven as of a mighty rushing wind, ... there appeared unto them cloven tongues ... And they were all filled with the Holy Ghost" (Acts 2:2-4). It was then the preaching of the Gospel and the building of the Church began for they all ran out into the streets and began to witness for Jesus. As a result, 3,000 souls believed and others were added daily. At Peter's second sermon, about 5,000 believed. The Holy Spirit was present to build the Church in Jesus' name and He has left us a record for our guidance in the Acts and Epistles of the methods He taught them to use.

Jesus had said in John, "He shall glorify me: for He shall receive of mine, and shall shew *it* unto you" (16:14). What was it that He would receive and show? Of Jesus' triumph, at His resurrection, it is said, "he led captivity captive and gave gifts unto men" (Eph 4:8), and in Psalms (68:18), "thou hast received gifts for men." These He put in the power of the Holy Spirit, His Executive, and said of Him, "he will not speak of himself ... he will shew you things to come" (John 16:13). Just as Jesus, in self-effacement, came to show us the Father, so the Holy Spirit has come in self-effacement to show us the Son.

Abraham's Unnamed Servant: A Type of the Holy Spirit Seeking the Bride for Christ

There is a very beautiful picture of this truth in Genesis (Chapter 24), where the unnamed servant who is in charge of all that Abraham has, goes forth to seek a bride for Abraham's son. He has but one purpose, to seek a bride for Isaac. He says nothing of his own importance but simply, "I *am* Abraham's servant." He tells of the greatness of Abraham.

The Lord hath blessed my master greatly; and he is become great: and he hath given him flocks, and herds, and silver, and gold, and menservants, and maidservants, and camels and asses. And Sarah my master's wife bare a son to my master when she was old: (a child of miraculous birth – author's addition), and unto him hath he given all that he hath (Gen 24:35-36).

And just as Abraham and Isaac had given power over all their goods to the servant, "All the goods of his master were in his hand" (Gen 24:10), so the Holy Spirit glorifies Jesus by building for Him, His Church, dividing to every man severally as He wills, the gifts that Jesus received for men.

It is clear then that the Holy Spirit is the builder of the Church, in the name of and for Christ. This is the definite purpose He has in coming into the world, fitly exemplified by the servant who could neither eat nor accept other hospitality until assured that his master would be dealt with "kindly and truly" (Gen 24:49). When the maiden at the well dealt "kindly and truly," gifts were given, and when Laban dealt "kindly and truly," other gifts were given.

CHAPTER III

The Gifts of the Spirit

Not to Be Confused with Natural Talents

The Holy Spirit is ordained of God to be the builder of the Church and as He is a jealous God, jealous for the glory of Jehovah Jesus, He will not give this charge to another. To this day, He personally calls the workers, directs the work, and divides the gifts. How near we may be to grieving Him, when we thoughtlessly speak of "my work, my schools, my teachers, my evangelists," or lightly of any of the gifts He has received from Jesus with which to enable the Church in her conflict in the world.

In Building the Church the Holy Spirit Gives Both Fruit Gifts and Service Gifts

The former, fruit gifts, are listed in Galatians: love, joy, peace, longsuffering, gentleness, goodness, faith, meekness and temperance (5:22-23). Commenting on these, an eminent teacher of Scripture says:

> Christian character is not mere moral or legal correctness, but the possession and manifestation of nine graces. Love, joy, peace which is character as an inward state. Longsuffering, gentleness, goodness which is character in expression toward man, and faith, meekness, and temperance which is character in expression toward God. Taken together they present a moral portrait of Christ, and may be taken as the apostle's explanation of Gal. 2:20, "Not I but Christ" and as a definition of fruit in John 15:1-8. This character is possible because of the believer's vital union to Christ (John 15:5; 1 Cor. 12:12, 13), and is wholly the fruit of the Spirit in those believers who are yielded to Him.[2]

These are the fruit, not fruits, of the Spirit. Wherever the Spirit controls a life, all these nine graces appear. They are given when the Spirit comes at conversion and we grow in grace as we walk with God.

Service Gifts

The service gifts are revealed in 1 Corinthians (12:8-10): wisdom, knowledge, faith, healing, miracles, prophecy,

---

2. Cyrus I. Scofield, Cyrus I. Scofield Reference Bible. London, Oxford University Press, 1917.

discerning of spirits, tongues and interpretation of tongues. Chapters 12, 13 and 14 are a connected treatise by the Apostle Paul on these gifts. Chapter 12 concerns the operations of the Spirit in relation to the body of Christ. The Spirit forms the body by uniting believers to Christ and so to each other. Chapter 13 shows the uselessness of the gifts without love, definitely mentioning five of the nine. Chapter 14 speaks of their desirability, and especially of the place of the gift of tongues in the assembly. The gifts are equally honorable because they are "bestowed by the same Spirit, administered under the same Lord and energized by the same God."[3] The exhortation is made to "Covet earnestly the best gifts" in Chapter 12:31, and to "desire spiritual gifts" in Chapter 14:1. Each believer receives a spiritual enablement for specific service. None is destitute of such gifting but the Holy Spirit acts in complete sovereignty in their distribution (1 Cor 12:7, 11, 27). The exhortation of Paul to Timothy to "stir up the gift of God, which is in thee" (2 Tim 1:6), and "Neglect not the gift that is in thee" (1 Tim 4:14), suggests that even in ministers, the gift received needs cultivation.

As the Spirit is before us, in action, building the Church and dispensing the gifts, it is stated, "Now ye are the body of Christ, and members in particular" (1 Cor 12:27) and God hath set the members in the Church as it hath pleased Him. God gives the gifts and sets those to whom they are given, in the Church. The matter is of such importance that the work is not delegated. It is by virtue of the possession of the gift that the office is given and not vice versa. All are necessary. "The eye cannot say to the hand, I have no need of thee" (1 Cor 12:21).

---

3. Ibid.

Movements of the Holy Spirit

There have been Movements of the Holy Spirit, both in home and mission lands, that were not to be classified with the modern revival where the young converts are received into a fully organized church, the responsibility for which is in the hands of others and little is expected of them beyond participation in the regular program. These movements were occasions where convictions and circumstances forced the formation of a distinctively new church where new ground had to be broken, and impossibilities faced all. In such straits, men were driven to prayer for help and miracles happened. The Holy Spirit divided to every man severally, the gifts by means of which alone Christ's body the Church can function. Preachers and other orders sprang from most unlikely timber and, were we to examine what happened in the light of the Word, we would see that to one was given, by the Spirit:

> … the word of wisdom; to another the word of knowledge by the same Spirit; To another faith by the same Spirit; to another the gifts of healing by the same Spirit (for there were those who had a special burden and faith to pray for the sick – author's addition); To another the working of miracles (and miracles happened); to another prophecy; to another discerning of spirits (to discern where that which is of God ends and that which is of Satan begins – author's addition) (1 Cor 12:8-10).

With these enduements of the Holy Spirit, our fathers were familiar. Alas! that their children should lack them.

For our study, there remains two gifts in St. Paul's list that we may not cravenly leave out. These are the gift of tongues and the interpretation of tongues. Throughout the centuries, there may have been incidences of their appearance in the great revival movements, but generally they have not been encouraged, the attitude of Bible teachers having been, perhaps quite generally, that these spiritual gifts have ceased.

The Apostle acknowledged these two gifts and thanked God that he spoke with tongues more than the others, but he required interpretation, either by the speaker or an interpreter who might be present. If there was no interpreter, he required that he "keep silence in the church" (1 Cor 14:28). On the other hand, he commanded, "forbid not to speak with tongues" (1 Cor 14:39).

In speaking of the practices of even false religions, idle witticisms are not fitting, "For who maketh thee to differ *from another*? and what has thou that thou didst not receive?" (1 Cor 4:7). But in speaking of the gifts of the Holy Spirit, to the Church, whether they have ceased or not, we are on holy ground and holy men remove their shoes.

CHAPTER IV

The Church Inaugurated

At Pentecost, the Holy Spirit began to build the Church by giving the gifts by means of which, through the power of the Holy Spirit, it could accomplish its warfare "against principalities, against powers, against the rulers of the darkness of this world, against spiritual wickedness in high *places*" (Eph 6:12). Those on whom the tongues of fire sat, and who were all filled with the Holy Ghost (Acts 2:3-4), went out to witness publicly, as every follower of the Lord should do, and when the multitude came together, Peter stood up with the eleven. Here we see the Holy Spirit choosing Peter and giving him the gift of prophesy with unction, so that he was enabled to speak with conviction and to interpret, with authority, the prophecy of Joel. He was a chosen vessel unto God and his testimony added about 3,000 souls unto them.

Just what gifts, other than speaking with tongues, the others received is not revealed, but as Peter and John went up together into the temple and encountered the lame man (Acts 3:1-2), it becomes evident that Peter had received a gift of healing. Jesus had given the disciples power to heal, but He had departed and sent the Holy Spirit, who was now in charge of the new dispensation of grace. After the healing of the lame man, "all the people ran together unto them" (Acts 3:11), and Peter again used his newly received gift with unction and authority so that about 5,000 believed. This was followed by the arrest of Peter and John, and the use by Peter of his gift of preaching on the following day before the council. Here the boldness of John is mentioned, and doubtless, like all the others, he bore a fearless witness, but still Peter was leading. On being set free, they went to their own company, reported and prayed, "Now, Lord, ... grant ... that with all boldness they may speak the word, By stretching forth thine hand to heal; and that signs and wonders may be done" (Acts 4:29-30). Here is definite united prayer for the gifts of healing as well as for other gifts that may be classified under "Signs and Wonders."

As if to record that their prayers were answered, there follows the miracle of the death of Ananias and Sapphira, and the statement in Acts, that "by the hands of the apostles were many signs and wonders wrought" (5:12). This statement is followed by the statements below.

Insomuch that they brought forth the sick into the streets, and laid *them* on beds and couches, that at the least the shadow of Peter passing by might overshadow some of them. There also came a multitude *out* of the cities round about Jerusalem, bringing sick folks, and them that were vexed with unclean spirits: and they were healed every one (Acts 5:15-16).

Philip

In Acts 8:5-7, it is recorded that Philip used the gifts of preaching, miracles and of healing, and in his experience with the Ethiopian, "the word of wisdom." Then follows the conversion of Saul and in Acts 9:17-18, his being filled with the Holy Ghost, and baptism.

Paul

It remained for Paul to give us most of the knowledge we have in church planting and to set forth in 1 Cor 12-14), the gifts with which the Holy Spirit endows the Church. He records that:

> "… to one is given by the Spirit the word of wisdom; to another the word of knowledge by the same Spirit; to another faith by the same Spirit; to another gifts of healing by the same Spirit; to another the working of miracles; to another prophesy; to another discerning of spirits; to another *divers* kinds of tongues; to another the interpretation of tongues" (Acts 12:8-10).

There had to be order, "And God hath set some in the church, first apostles, secondarily prophets, thirdly teachers, after that miracles, then gifts of healings, helps, governments, diversities of tongues" (1 Cor 12:28). Those who have been endued with gifts and "set" in the Church by the Holy Spirit are given to the several churches, "he gave to some (churches), apostles; and some, prophets; and some, evangelists; and some, pastors and teachers" (Eph 4:11).

It was because of this divine pattern, these spiritual gifts and enablements, so fully directed by the Holy Spirit, that the early churches were able to, so soon, be given deacons and elders and that they not only looked after their own local churches but carried the Gospel to other parts, thus permitting the missionaries (the apostles and evangelists) to open new fields. Even those who were unlearned and ignorant, former idolaters and slaves, with these enablements of the Holy Spirit, did then, and have since, when permitted to do so, carried forward devotedly the work of God. In Madagascar, the missionaries found, after an enforced absence of twenty-five years that the Church had doubled. After Protestant missionaries were expelled from Ethiopia under the Mussolini regime and were subsequently re-admitted, they were amazed to find a gracious movement of the Holy Spirit in progress in which native Ethiopians were leading and scores of thousands had been saved.

Doubtless, it is the first work of modern missions to give the young churches a trained ministry, but we leave the New Testament pattern when we usurp their place as pastors and confine them to the place of helpers and servants and that for decades or a century.

CHAPTER V

The Mission Temporary – The Church Permanent

Had I been asked, when, as a young man of twenty-three years, I found myself on the way to Portuguese East Africa, just what my purpose in going was, I would, no doubt, have replied, "to preach the Gospel to the heathen." It is doubtful if the Church that sent me had any clearer conception of the purpose of my going. This lack of instruction in, or failure to perceive, the purpose of missions clearly, has been at the root of much misdirected effort that could have been used of the Holy Spirit mightily, to save the world.

The purpose of Jesus in coming to die for men was to

build the Church. "I will build my Church" said He, (Matt 16:18). It is His body, in the world, against which the gates of hell shall not prevail, and through which He does His work. We are strangely mission-minded. We are going to build or found a mission among some foreign speaking people with strange customs, not realizing that we will be the foreigners with foreign customs, often being in the delicate position of being uninvited guests. Should we not rather, like our Master, build the Church? So confused may our thinking become on this matter, that if dissatisfied with the methods we see, we set for ourselves, to build "a self-supporting mission", still not taught that it is only the Church that can become self-supporting, and more than self-supporting, self-governing and self-propagating.

The relative position of Church and mission should be clearly in our minds before we begin to build. God calls the Church, any and every Church saying, "Go ye therefore, and teach all nations" (Matt 28:19). Each Church can only go by sending representatives, and these, God the Holy Spirit calls, for "no man taketh this honor unto himself, but he that is called of God, as *was* Aaron" (Heb 5:4). These representatives are the legitimate burden of the Church that sends them and should be supported by it, even as Paul says, "ye sent once and again to my necessity" (Phil 4:16). These missionaries and their activities are referred to as the mission.

The Church

The purpose of the mission is, or should be, in the divine economy, to plant Churches. It does this by preaching the Gospel for "it pleased God by the foolishness of preaching to save them that believe" (1 Cor 1:21). Those who believe may have been, in their unsaved state, as unlikely material from which to build a Church as were the Corinthians of whom Paul wrote in 1 Corinthians:

> "Know ye not that the unrighteous shall not inherit the kingdom of God? Be not deceived: neither fornicators, nor idolators, nor adulterers, nor effeminate, nor abusers of themselves with mankind, Nor thieves, nor covetous, nor drunkards, nor revilers, nor extortioners, shall inherit the kingdom of God. And such were some of you: but ye are washed, but ye are sanctified, but ye are justified in the name of the Lord Jesus, and by the Spirit of our God" (1 Cor 6:9-11).

After they have undergone this process of cleansing, and the Holy Spirit has divided the gifts "unto every man severally as he will" (1 Cor 12:8-11), He is able to build of them His Church; "a spiritual house, an holy priesthood, to offer up spiritual sacrifices, acceptable to God by Jesus Christ" (1 Pet 2:5).

Of them He says, "Now ye are the body of Christ, and members in particular. And God hath set some in the church, first apostles, secondarily prophets, thirdly teachers, after that miracles, then gifts of healings, helps, governments, diversities of tongues" (1 Cor 12:27-28). Here we see the Holy Spirit enduing the Church with gifts and enablements for its work. In Ephesians, we learn that the persons who have been so endowed are themselves the gifts given to various churches, "For the perfecting of the saints, for the work of the ministry, for the edifying of the body of Christ: Till we all come in the unity of the faith, and of the knowledge of the Son of God, unto a perfect man, unto the measure of the stature of the fullness of Christ" (Eph 4:12-13).

God's Method

The Holy Spirit called the Church to send missionaries and He called and sent the missionaries. "How shall they hear without a preacher? And how shall they preach except they be sent?" (Rom 10:14-15). He who calls and sends the missionary to preach, convicts, washes, sanctifies, justifies, fills with the Holy Spirit and enables, by gifts, those who believe and so sets orders in the young church, thus building it into "an holy temple in the Lord: In whom ye also are builded together for an habitation of God through the Spirit" (Eph 2:21-22).

Living Stones

Again, the figure of a temple is used, *"ye are* God's building" (1 Cor 3:9). "Coming, *as unto* a living stone ... Ye also, as living stones, are built up a spiritual house" (1 2:4-5). The Holy Spirit is the builder who shapes the living stones and fits them into the spiritual house, the Church.

There is no hard and fast boundary between the young Church and the mission, any more than there is in a family. At first the parents are the kindly guides and helpers, but it is well understood that in a few short years the children will attain their majority, each child is entrusted with a charge in the family, from a very early age. Long before they are mature, they are taken into the councils of the family and so, without discord, not to say disruption, the understanding parents pass on to their children, the position they, at first, exclusively held. Similarly the missionaries are, at first, leading, but very soon begin to take council with nationals. With the acquisition of converts, the simpler forms of Church councils begin to function; in Methodism first the society meeting, then the official board or local church council, then the quarterly and annual conferences. The missionaries are full members of these several bodies and so are free to accept any service to which the Church may appoint them. At the same time, they retain their membership in their home denomination so that they may have a Church home when their service is no longer needed abroad. They maintain leadership in the Church not by any right, as missionaries, but by the Spirit of Christ in service. The Church increases and the mission decreases. There are no throes of devolution, for all this was foreseen and planned, as in the case of a wise and loving family.

Institutions

In regions beyond, the first work of the missionary is to preach and teach as we find Paul doing. When converts have been made they all bear witness, and to prepare them for witnessing and leadership becomes the first work of the missionary. Jesus early called the twelve, and in the school of experience, taught them in anticipation of the day when He would turn over the work to them. Paul followed the same plan. Their methods of accomplishing this were effectual and succeeded, but did not encumber their followers. Such was their understanding of the Gospel of Christ, and the power of the Spirit, actuating it that with a paucity of equipment, they achieved the maximum in fruitage by using every convert in the full measure of the gift with which they had been endued.

Perhaps institutions have caused more discord between missions and young Churches than any other single factor. In their great desire to help backward peoples, missions have aimed to provide them with "the best training possible". To them, this meant replicas of the fine schools in which they were taught. As the low economy of their people made it impossible for them to build and equip such expensive plants, the mission supplied everything for them. After so generous a gesture, by every rule (except the golden rule), the mission should govern and the people accept it all with thankfulness. They do so for a time. When they have been taught and are competent to undertake the responsibility they desire to, they not only take over the training institutions, but also their whole church program, for not only the responsibility, but the right to evangelize a land, belongs to the Church of that land. To aliens it may be given to introduce the Gospel and to help the young Church but not to lord it over them even in the economic sphere.

It has happened that after leaders had been taught, the young Church, feeling the call of God to help its own people, and being financially unable to support these institutions, built and operated on a western economy, has pressed the missions to endow them permanently and turn them over. How effectually this would encumber the home Church in its effort to obey the Lord's command to "go," need not be stressed, and yet the young Church was inextricably entangled by the program of its founders. The moral is that the mission, from the beginning, should foresee its own retirement and institute nothing that the young Church will not be able to carry, eventually. The International Missionary Council in its paper, "The Witness of a Revolutionary Church" (1947) after its Whitby conference, includes among its findings: "From the beginning of an evangelistic task in a new area, the aim must be the bringing into existence at the earliest possible date of a self-governing and self-propagating Church and every effort must be made to make the period of tutelage as short as possible."[4]

In his book, *The Church in the New Jamaica* by J. Merle Davis (1942), there is an interesting description of the methods of work employed by the Adventist mission. They began operations in several places among people of the lowest

---

4. Stephen Neill, "The Witness of a Revolutionary Church," *International Review of Mission*, Vol 36 (4) October 1947, 434-451.

economy. When there were converts, the tithe was taught and required, as an integral part of the Gospel. The mother church in America bought a small farm and built a modes training school with a well-equipped bakery and workshops. Pupils were given work on the farm and in the shops and from the current income they were paid by the hour. From their wages they paid for their board, books and tuition. Aside from the salaries of three missionaries, the institution was self-supporting and presented no financial obstacle to the autonomy of the new Church. After 42 years, there were 137 organized churches served by 17 trained, ordained national pastors and 10,515 baptized members. Only three missionaries remained, those in the training school, the others having been set free to open new work.

The Love of Christ Constrains the Church

Where peoples are living on a lower economy than that to which we are accustomed (and that is everywhere), it becomes our duty to introduce with the Gospel, a system of church economy that they can finance. If we build on our economy and make their Church to be dependent on foreign funds, we have unfairly bound the young Church with the Gospel that is intended to make men free. It has been amply demonstrated in Apostolic and in modern times and in many lands, that there are no people so poor that they cannot propagate and sustain their Church in their own way. A student of mission economy of worldwide experience has said the following:

> A common assumption with regard to peoples of lower economic standards, and particularly to a society based upon a subsistence economy, is that they lack the economic and cultural resources required for supporting the Church of Christ. Such

an assumption is based upon a mistaken concept of
the Church and a failure to recognize fully the inner
capacity and available resources of races which have
a different cultural heritage and economy. The way
of redemption which God has provided is essentially
not too costly nor too heavy a burden to be carried
by any of His children, no matter how much they
lack the economic and social amenities to which
a European civilization has become accustomed.
There is evidence in the record of missions that some
of the most primitive and backward peoples have
been the first to develop an indigenous and
financially independent Church and, on the other
hand, it is among races whose economic level and
culture most nearly approximate those of the
mission-sending lands that support of the Church has
been most difficult to achieve.[5]

It is for us to remember that the methods of propagating the Gospel, to which we are accustomed, were not those of the early Church. They worshipped in a house or by the river-side or in some shelter of their own construction. The elders and deacons of each congregation were local people, presumably with their own means of support, who were sometimes given love gifts by the Church (1 Tim 5:17).

Lay Workers

Methodism followed this example. Instead of appointing a full time, paid pastor for every congregation, it organized

---

5. J. Merle Davis, *The Church in the New Jamaica: A Study of the Economic and Social Basis of the Evangelical Church in Jamaica.* New York: Department of Social and Economic Research and Counsel, International Missionary Council, 1942, 31.

"circuits" with one paid pastor for several, perhaps a score or more of preaching places. The pioneering circuit rider of the last century was of this order. The system drew heavily and successfully on laymen to shepherd the flock. There were lay or local preachers, lay exhorters, lay class leaders, stewards, deaconesses and Sunday School workers. There was scarcely a family in Methodism that was not spiritually enriched by some form of voluntary work for the Church. Their constant, prayerful care, their house-to-house visitation, seeking the lost, sick and straying, consolidated and maintained the gains, while their preachers, the mighty evangelists like Wesley himself, opened new areas. Such a system will work on mission fields, even among peoples of a subsistence economy. Let them build their church buildings and schools when they feel the need, according to their own economy. One of the main criticisms by the Indian people, of the British regime in India, was that they could govern the country at a fraction of the cost and they are proving it.

Islam has established itself over vast areas in Africa by the simple method of each trader being a missionary. He teaches a group who, with him, build a place for prayer and school and carry on their own work, and open new places without outside help. The idol worshippers of the East have been trained to give for their false religions, sufficient to propagate the Gospel, were it used in that way. Could we be patient and direct their efforts indigenously, the advance of the Gospel would not be in almost exact ratio to the amount of money that could be secured for them in a foreign country.

Lowliness

Do aliens have the right, either as emissaries of the Church or otherwise, to bind a people by so fusing their western economy with the Gospel they propagate that they cannot, in measurable distance, be free from western help and western influence? The east gave us the simple, sweet Gospel of the grace of God. Do we return it to them so vastly improved as to be no longer eastern and within their economy? Must we learn from Islam or godless communism that which we could have learned from our own Scriptures? O' for getting back to the simplicity of the life of Jesus and of His cross, by whom, Paul could say, "the world is crucified unto me, and I unto the world" (Gal 6:14). Whatever the spiritual state of Mahatma Gandhi may have been, he gave the world a glimpse of lowliness that, admittedly, he found in Jesus. He stooped to conquer.

> Several of Mahatma Gandhi's lieutenants are Christian young men who have come out of well-known Christian colleges and have served as ministers or Y.M.C.A. secretaries. They have found in the life of simplicity and economic renunciation that surrounds the Mahatma a satisfaction and peace that the atmosphere of large material institutions and comfortable salaries did not provide.
> One of them said:
> "The life and example of Jesus has a powerful appeal to us Indians. Christ of the New Testament fits into Indian life and gains a response from the Indian heart, but it is different with the Christ of Europe and America who comes with an institutionalized Church, with imposing mission compounds, with high-salaried workers, with palatial Christian colleges. We find it hard to see Jesus in all this display of economic power and pomp. Moreover, the economic lure becomes very strong to the indigent Indian when Christ is presented in this setting.

> Some of us who are products of this system have experienced a revulsion from it and have returned to an Indianized interpretation of religious service. We believe that this is nearer the real spirit of Christ than that which is embodied in the marble halls of the Christian college, and in salaries that are many times the income of the common people."[6]

The speaker sat on the mud floor of a mud-walled, grass thatched hut. There were no chairs or tables or modern comforts. A little group of such huts, often referred to as "the real capital of India," formed the Mahatma's headquarters and lent sincerity to the speaker's words.

CHAPTER VI

Teaching Them

Every Missionary A Teacher

It is not difficult for a missionary dealing with a "revolutionary Church," to see that wrong methods were used in its planting. He is convinced that most of his troubles stem from the wrong use of mission money. In his Guide Book, he sees that his difficulties are not those of Paul. He put responsibility on the Church as soon as the Holy Spirit had chosen, and by service gifts, enabled local leaders to become its "overseers" (Acts 20:28). Paul did not finance them. He visited them, wrote letters to them, sent messengers to them, prayed for them and bore a burden for them, "the care of all the Churches" (2 Cor 11:28), but he left them in the keeping of elders set over them by the Holy Spirit, and passed on.

---

6. J. Merle Davis, *The Economic Basis of the Church,* Oxford University Press, 1939, 151-152.

Missionaries Not Pastors

A missionary remaining as pastor of a national Church, decade after decade, sets aside New Testament order. Where this is done, invariably, it is the use of foreign money that makes it possible. By its means, a foreign missionary may hold the office but finds it necessary to use "assistants" or the so-called "evangelists", (their service is really that of a pastor), who do the real shepherding. They are expected to report any who walk disorderly to the foreign pastor, but the people resent this and are able to bring strong pressure on them to not align themselves with aliens, against their own people. When this is known to the missionary, his faith in the leaders of the Church is shaken, a vital matter. Like every system that does not follow the Book, it is found wanting. The elders of the Acts were members of the Church, made overseers by the Holy Spirit and maintained, according to their needs by it. Human arrangements supported by foreign money, lands or other economic bolstering, invariably prove to be an entanglement.

A special function of all missionaries, evangelical, educational or medical, in planting the Church is to teach. This is, in embryo, their whole purpose and function. The Church will need a trained ministry and perhaps teachers and medical doctors. To supply these needs, as we are able, is the task to which we are devoted.

Evangelical missionaries should be especially committed to the developing of a holy, taught ministry for the Church that God the Holy Spirit builds. In doing this they will, of necessity, preach the Gospel. This is their first laboratory method. All their converts will be empowered of the Spirit to be witnesses as all were at Pentecost, for "the manifestation of the Spirit is given to every man to profit withal" (1 Cor 12:7). It will soon be evident that God has set some in the Church as prophets, teachers, helps and governments, not to mention the other five services. If lacking, these endowments should be sought by earnest, persevering prayer, for only by their means can a Church be built, and by their means unlearned and ignorant men can and do become mighty leaders. Two or more of these will be the Spirit-appointed overseers of the congregation. Having their own living, the question of support does not enter in. All will witness publicly and privately. When the group needs a full-time pastor or want to send out an evangelist as their missionary, they should make their own financial arrangements. It will greatly help them, if the missionary makes it clear that the mission will not help them with money. Otherwise, the incentive to give for the spread of the Gospel is lost, for seeing on every hand evidence that the mission is rich, why should they support or send out workers? In his book, *Can Organized Religion Survive*, Dr. Oswald Smith says the following:

> I found foreign missionaries acting as pastors of native churches, a thing unknown in Scripture. God never sent them out to localize their efforts by becoming pastors of native churches. The business, the one and only business of the foreign missionary is to train native workers and put responsibility upon them. They should be appointed as evangelists or teachers, according to their gifts, and sent forth to evangelize their country. They should be ordained as pastors and elders and placed in charge of churches. Each church should be self-governing, and like a hive it should repeatedly swarm. God will raise up a native pastor much more qualified than himself, (the missionary), to take charge of the work which he founds. It is up to him to keep the vision of

evangelization before all the churches so that they will multiply on every side.[7]

The evangelical missionary then, has his true work before him, namely to train a holy ministry endowed with the gifts of the Spirit for the Church that is being called out. This is the foremost of present-day tasks. Like our Lord, he will teach them many things in preaching and practice, and like our Lord he will send them out, after a period of instruction, to active pastoral work for a time. When they are brought back, they will report on their work, be reproved, rebuked or exhorted and further taught before being sent again to preach. They should not be sheltered too much for faith grows in the test and in adversity. The Church must have a full voice in all the arrangements. Let them feel that the work is theirs and that God requires of them that they evangelize their people.

It is well known that deep unrest exists over much of Asia and Africa with deep resentment for Europeans and their systems of government. "Europeans out of Asia" is a powerful slogan. To meet this, there has been a sincere effort in some areas to definitely prepare the Africans for self-government. The Governor of French Equatorial Africa has been an African Negro. The Kings of Ruanda and Urundi have been taught and are retained in the Belgian system, and the Chiefs are being trained to exercise authority under them. In East Africa, the British Government has declared that it regards itself as Trustee for the African peoples, and that if the interests of the African peoples and those of the Europeans resident in the colonies, are antagonistic one to the other, the interests of the Africans must prevail.

In Anglo-Egyptian Sudan the Nilotic tribes have, in past ages, paid little attention to the struggles over their land by

---

7. Oswald J. Smith, "What's Wrong on the Mission Field," *Can Organized Religion Survive?*, Toronto, Toronto Tabernacle Press. 1932, 46-47.

foreign powers except to defend themselves from attack, but as in Africa generally, lately a remarkable change has come over the Shilluks, the Dinkas, the Nuers and especially, to the tribes farther north. The British have put Sudanese understudies at their sides from the capital at Khartoum to the remotest district commissioner's office. This is in preparation for self-rule and in addition, native doctors and nurses are being taught in the hospitals and native engineers on Nile steamboats. Water from the Sennar dam has made possible the planting of a million acres of cotton, and projected dams will irrigate other millions of acres of land that eventually, the Sudanese may in the end rule. In others areas, in the realms of both Church and State, safety is still sought in repression and segregation.

    The hope of the Church in a political upheaval would be a holy, taught, ordained African Clergy leading the Church. This would form a rallying point for all Christians and be the only possible check to the excesses of political, revolutionary leaders. To train and install such a Ministry is the most urgent task of missions. Some societies are well along this road with a trained Clergy and an African Bishop here and there, while others still fear to ordain African Deacons and Elders. The Roman Catholic Church, always ahead in strategy, has recently announced the formation of three new hierarchies in Africa, the first in fourteen centuries. In these three hierarchies, there will be a total of three archbishops and eleven bishops. A Vatican authority makes the pronouncement that, "In areas where there are forty white missionary priests and only four native priests the choice of bishop will probably go to the white priest … but where there are forty native priests and forty missionaries it is probable that one of the native clergy will be chosen… For the time being, the white bishops now there will remain at their posts as members of the new hierarchies, but local Negro priests, if considered qualified are expected to fill vacancies."[8] This move is expected to mean a rapid expansion of the number of African Negro Catholic Bishops, and, at least in theory, increases the possibility of the election of a Negro Pope. A Vatican authority states that at least two Negroes have been Popes during the first five centuries of the Christian era, but that white Europeans have predominated in that office for more than a thousand years.[9]

Just as the Roman Catholic Church has indigenized its former missionary areas of North America and the Latin Republics, getting the roots of the new Church well down into the soil under its feet, for temporal support, so now in Africa, a more recent missionary area, the same process is at work and will produce the same results. If the African Church can see that its leaders are an equal brotherhood with the white missionaries, and that a trained, ordained African ministry is being built up to succeed the white missionaries, they will respond to any call to sacrifice for the Lord. But if after fifty years, all the authority is in the hands of the whites, they should not be disappointed if Africans are hesitant about offering themselves for the posts that retard the Church in its desire to have a ministry that proceeds from themselves, which they can support and work together with just as white Churches do.

In primitive Urundi, after twenty-six years, two of their big missions with cathedrals to accommodate over 2,000 people and commodious chapels, the white priests had already gone to build similar institutions elsewhere in the land. Their places were taken by African priests, for they had not neglected to establish seminaries to train them. The Bishop was still a white man. But they had taken Congolese seminary trained men to Rome, and given them, through the medium

---

8. See Pope Pius XII, Evangelii Praecones, Acta Apostolicae Sedis, AAS, 1951.
9. Ibid.

of education or ordination, the very highest orders given by the Roman Catholic Church, and then had graduated, some of them with honors. They will need Cardinals in Africa, some day, and perhaps a Pope as has already been suggested. In the light of this, how retarded is the program of many Protestant denominations?

Missionary Teachers

Similarly, missionaries who go out as teachers cannot aim at instructing, directly, whole populations, but they can raise up teachers who would be available to their people for this purpose. Nor is it their responsibility to support them all. In the beginnings of primitive work, it often happens that the teacher spends no more time in teaching than the adult population do in learning. If he has his means of livelihood, he should be glad to do this as a service for his Lord, until his people, being prompted by the Holy Spirit, give him love gifts in accordance to Galatians, "Let him that is taught in the word communicate unto him that teacheth in all good things" (Gal 6:6). A small school fee from each pupil might suffice. It is this principle of using local, unpaid people to teach that Frank Laubach[10] has sponsored with revolutionary effect among illiterate peoples.

But it is the higher schools and colleges on the mission fields that have caused the deepest heart burning to the missions and resentment to the Church. Institutions are essential to a trained leadership but the impartation of

---

10. Frank Charles Laubach (1884-1970) was a Congregational Christian missionary who was deeply concerned about poverty, injustice and illiteracy. He became known as the "Apostle to the Illiterates." Working in the Philippines, he developed the "Each One Teach One" literacy program. In appreciation of Laubach teaching old people how to read and write, the tribes of Belgian Congo called him Okombekombe which means "mender of old baskets."

knowledge is not inseparably bound up with marble halls. The ample pages of knowledge, "rich with the spoils of time,"[11] have been unrolled before the eyes of the East for centuries, with the minimum of equipment, at the feet of a Gamaliel.[12] To so en-fetter learning as to render it immobile without subsidy from a foreign source for its initiation and perpetuation, notwithstanding the sincerity of our purpose, is to humble a people, blight their future prospects and leave them bound where they should be free. Before an institution is begun, the nationals who must eventually inherit and operate it, should be taken into the mission councils and a serious effort made to work out a plan whereby the Church may be able to finance it when national leaders have been sufficiently trained. Their representatives should sit on the institutional committee from the beginning, for they can give much pertinent advice and they are profoundly interested. From such institutions, already in operation, in different mission lands, a fund of information could be gathered.

Medical Missionaries

Medical missionaries are also teachers. Their task is not only to relieve and cure. If millions of people must wait till churches in other countries send them sufficient doctors and nurses to care for their sick and build hospitals for them, their case is hopeless. Logically, the task is to train nurses, male and female, and where possible, assisted by the government, certificated, national doctors. To do this they must have hospitals where they relieve and cure. If those they train will have to practice in the bush under primitive conditions, this condition must be reflected in their training. During the war,

---

11. from Thomas Gray's *Elegy Written in a Country Churchyard*, 1751.
12. In the Christian tradition, Gamaliel was a first century Jewish teacher, member of the Sanhedrin, and instructor of Paul the Apostle.

surgeons found that a lot of good work could be done in tents and barns.

In Belgian Congo, the government and the missions are working together to provide an African, trained, medical staff. While this is being developed, partially trained Africans are in charge of "rural dispensaries" where they treat thousands of simpler ailments. Difficult cases go to the European doctors at the hospitals.

In the French Camaroons, mission trained, African doctors who have not yet been recognized by the government, have posts in the rural areas where they relieve much suffering and perform many major operations. This is permissible, professionally, because the mission doctor in the area is recognized by the government and these are classed as his helpers. The University of Witwatersrand in South Africa is now graduating African medical doctors.

Backward peoples are accustomed to paying their herbalists and spirit doctors well, and do not object to paying a reasonable fee for medicines and nursing. The blessing is that they are able to secure honest and skilled medical aid, in their need, and at a price within their economy, rather than that a few can be cared for gratuitously. Such fees go a long way toward meeting the expense of a dispensary or hospital, and as this is an integral part of the training of the student doctors, it should, in some sense, help to establish a code of morals, restraining avarice, should it occur in so high a calling, and, on the other hand, provide an income that would serve the turn of men whose living would necessarily be above that of the average man.

In Ruanda-Urundi, where the missions work together in an Alliance, each hospital staff trains a class of young men as nurses. From these classes, certain promising ones are sent to a central hospital where they are given further training. From this Alliance training class, they go to a government school and on completion of the course receive a diploma. They can then be employed in the government medical service, or in mission hospitals, which are also a part of the government service, being subsidized and directed by it. The government plan, which is being accelerated, is to provide a rural dispensary, with one or more trained dispensers, at a distance of twelve miles apart, and a hospital at each government post. As African doctors are graduated, they will, doubtless, take the places of the dispensers.

The health of a people is a responsibility of government. Where this has been accepted and provided for, the missions are free for work that is peculiarly their own, and which the government cannot do; namely, to plant the Church.

CHAPTER VII

Finance

To fail to give the young Church a sound, workable financial plan could keep it in economic bondage to the mission indefinitely. God not only commanded tithes and offerings but gave minute instructions as to the time, place and manner of their presentation. Not only money, but produce and labor were given to God. In Central Africa the ticket system has been used, from the beginning at any new point, with great success. Each enquirer was given a small card with name and place on one side and openings for tithes on the other. As he desired to become a Christian, and a member of the Church, in due time, it was as necessary that he learn to support the Church as it was to learn the creed, before he was baptized. Otherwise, how could the Church survive? Baptism was not presented as an incentive to give, nor was any special thank offering asked at that time. Too often, after baptism, the candidate has ceased to give anything commensurate with his tithe. They were made to feel that the responsibility of carrying the Gospel to their own people was upon them, that the Church was God's plan to do this and it must be supported or it could do nothing. God's promised blessing on the tithe was stressed.

The leader for each group received the monthly offering, entered it on their tickets and brought offering and tickets to a district treasurer who had a book in which the data of the tickets for the entire district was kept under separate groups. He checked the money with the cards of each leader and entered the data for each person in his book. The money for the entire district was deposited in an iron box in which was kept a cash book for entries of the amounts of group receipts, and for payments. Two stewards, chosen by the Church, kept the keys of this box and were responsible for the money to the Church. The accounting was always done in public and the accounts were audited annually. Sometimes the cash in the box exceeded the amount shown in the books, but it was never short. They left the box at the mission house for safe-keeping but we had no key for it. The stewards often counted its contents to see if there was sufficient to make the monthly payments to the Preacher-teachers. If it was insufficient they called for any outstanding amounts or asked that payday be deferred a week.

The mission had definitely stated that it would neither give nor loan money for the salaries of the Pastor-teachers. They were the responsibility of the Church. This strengthened the hands of those who desired to build a self-supporting Church and enabled them to press for the tithe. They also learned that when giving fell off, the Church was becoming luke-warm and needed revival. In the early years, a missionary made out the pay sheet. They took this and their box and made the payments. However, the system was so simple that they soon mastered it.

On Wednesdays they brought the tithe of their produce. The stewards appraised it, entered in on the individual tickets and sold the produce. At bean harvest, the Church often stored the tithe in our gasoline drums and held it till the price rose. If the stewards allowed too much for produce they could not get back the full credit allowed on the tickets, and if they allowed too little, persons would sell their produce elsewhere and bring money, so in this way, the matter kept itself in adjustment. In an undernourished population, produce was always welcome and offerings of this kind produced a sense of fellowship that mere money did not give. In fact it was a weekly social event, the donor praising the produce and humorously demanding a little more and the Church representative good-humouredly dispraising it and pointing out the produce of another and citing the allowance given until all were agreed. The West may like "the use of one word in buying and selling," but that is not a Bible quotation. It would deprive the East of the social side of the market. The missionary may not fit into such a plan among another people, preferring to get it done and away to something else, but the East like it and, after all, why should not the East manage its own Church finance?

In addition to money and produce, they gave much labor in building their church and school buildings (often built with bricks they made themselves), and in assisting their pastor with his gardens. By this simple system, self-support and self-government were inculcated from the beginning and the young Church prepared for the day, should it ever come, which many a young Church has experienced, when war has left them without their missionaries, and without the money the missionaries unfailingly supplied. How much better that they should be taught to draw their temporal support from the ground under their feet and their spiritual support from the heaven over their heads, from the beginning? And how much better that a Church should come to full status, with the help of its missionaries, leaving them free to open new fields, as some missions do, than that war should force this status suddenly on mission and Church alike?

"A Root of All Evil"

There is no greater danger for the Church planter than money. Money divides men. If national pastors be paid by the mission, he is an exceptional dispenser of funds who can keep the idea of master and servant entirely out of the picture, a relationship entirely foreign to an equal brotherhood. It may even be considered necessary to retain this economic leverage in order to assure control of the workers under our leadership, who may be referred to as, "my evangelists" or "my teachers." But money control is the worst kind of control, and should have no place in the Church of Jesus Christ. The day for control by missionaries is past. With the rising tide of nationalism in the East and the slogan, "The white man out of Asia," the attitude of Jesus, "I am among you as he that serveth" (Luke 22:27), has a special significance.

Let Us Go On

In every saved heart there is felt, not only the urge to assist the local work, but also to contribute towards evangelism, at home and abroad. An African woman expressed this urge by going on foot to all the places the Church opened to witness for her Lord. When the Church united to send an offering to foreign countries, she said that her feet could not take her there so she wanted to send an offering, and so have a part in that work also. When the young Church began to send out missionaries, a home mission's treasury was created. Each district had adopted the system described above and had its own steel box that took the name of the district and its two

African treasurers or stewards. Now another box was added, to be named, "Twigir' Imbere" (i.e., Let Us Go On).

In this box was placed the tithe of the monthly, district receipts. The African missionaries immediately inaugurated the ticket system, they know so well. Each person wanting to learn was given a ticket and expected to give a tithe. The "Twigir' Imbere" treasury helped the missionaries to get to their fields and assisted them, if necessary, until the local income supplied their needs. Fear of being accused of using Church money made the treasurers hesitate to take office, at first, but as items were recorded in the presence of the congregation, or a group of people, and the accounts were audited, this fear passed and confidence took its place.

We are not suggesting that this plan is the perfect one to be used universally but we do believe that "The way of redemption which God has provided is essentially not too costly nor too heavy a burden to be carried by any of His children no matter how much they lack the social and economic amenities to which a European civilization has been accustomed" (Source unknown).

CHAPTER VIII

The Teacher Becomes the Taught

> "I am debtor ... both to the wise, and to the unwise"
> (Rom 1:14)

The new missionary, notwithstanding all his preparation, may well regard himself as a novice as he begins his new life; a stranger in a strange land. He understands neither language nor customs. His attitude towards national customs should be that society, even primitive society, responds in some way to its own needs, and that there is a reason, hidden away somewhere, for each custom. It is from these reasons, these basic beliefs, that conclusions, right or wrong, come. If we are teachers desirous of imparting truth, we must search out the reason for the custom. A custom, be it Chinese, Indian or African, is not necessarily a "heathen custom." Indeed, it would be well to forget the term "heathen." Could we not refer to customs as Chinese, Indian or African and so give to the custom the dignity of one of these great peoples, as did Paul on Mars Hill? (Acts 17:22-23), "Whom therefore ye ignorantly worship, him declare I unto you." If we would sit down patiently with some of their older men or women, and as humble learners ask them in a dignified and serious way, the reasons for a custom we do not understand, we might open a fountain of lore and philosophy that would be astounding, and put us in a place of understanding that would enable us to, as Paul did, let light shine unto them. Their respect for their parents might even be classed as a Christian virtue planted in their hearts by God Himself.

It would be neither useful nor Christian to hold up to ridicule the religion, however wrong, of any man, even that of the poor, deluded, African witch doctor. When sickness came, the primitive African peoples in their blindness (because we had not brought them the light), concluded that much of their trouble came from evil spirits that responded to the incantations of medicine men. The spirits were divided into two classes, friendly and malicious. If they were to be helped by the friendly and protected from the malicious, there must be priests to stand between spirits and men. Hence the witch doctor, the device of Satan. He was their only recourse and while he must have been a miserable comforter, he seems to have believed profoundly in himself and to have inspired faith in his consultants, so that the priesthood continued for centuries and he was regarded as the great friend of his people when trouble came. To rail at him will not help. To tell the people that they are deceived will not suffice. There is always someone to defend or excuse the doctor, even if they receive no better returns than the woman described in Mark 5:25-26. Luke gives the incident in much detail but being a physician himself, passes over the point made by Mark that she "rather grew worse" (see Luke 8:43-48). The sympathies of the people are with their medicine men and they will not give up what they have, however useless, until faith in Christ reveals the lie of Satan. The human heart turns mysteriously towards these uncertainties, as witness the thousands who follow them in our own lands.

The Native Question

Soon after I arrived in South Africa I came upon a new subject for study, in the press and in conversation under the caption, "the native question." I read widely in an effort to discover its meaning. It was commonly considered that the new comers did not understand it, which was understandable, but that the old timers, or those who had grown up in the country, did. As I was to work among natives, I felt it a duty to get to the bottom of it. There being no African press then, what I read was the teaching of Europeans. What the Africans them-selves said, on the subject, if they said anything, I did not know. I was inclined to think the Europeans were dealing fairly with their wards who seemed to be contented, happy and law-abiding.

The Country's Greatest Asset

As time went on I began to realize something of the tremendous contribution the Natives had made and were making towards the development of the country. Whatever advance was made, whether it was house-building, road or railroad construction, mining, farming or building of wharves or cities, the African furnished the labor for ALL. Labor saving machines had scarcely made their appearance as yet. "The boy and the barrow" were the equipment for road-building, to which was added the pick and shovel. Surely the Belgian Administration in Congo understands something of "the native problem" when it speaks of the native African as the greatest wealth of the country, and once a road has been constructed will no longer permit porterage, as it is a menace to the health and constancy of the population.

The Under Privileged

I found that in South Africa the Europeans had taken over the land by conquest and had set aside certain areas, known as Locations, notoriously insufficient for the needs of the Natives. In addition, Natives could live on the farms of white men by contracting to work under conditions incompatible with a free economy. Neither on the Locations nor the farms was the available acreage sufficient for their dwellings, agriculture and pasturage.

Access to the land is a crucial matter. The Africans being 85% of the population were reported to hold 15% of the land, while the Europeans being 15% of the population held 85% of the land. Some further acreage has since been allocated for Native occupation but only in very limited areas can Africans buy land. They are practically a landless people.

When in Southern Rhodesia, after conquest, the Matabele met Cecil Rhodes for a settlement and they complained, "The white man claims all the land." The reply was, "We will give you settlements. We will set apart locations for you. We will give you land." Pathetically, too weak for further resistance, they replied, "You will give us land in our own country!"

I began to feel that the "native question" could be visualized as how to get the most possible out of the Native for the smallest possible return. Years later when the Africans became vocal through their press they said, "There is no 'native problem.' We are in the land of our fathers. The problem is the European."

But if the government has retarded Native progress, some of the missions seem to be in the same category and are censured by the African intelligentsia. They have caustically remarked that we brought them the Book, but while they were reading it, we stole their land. There are denominations that have preached the Gospel, seen thousands saved, trained for them and ordained an African ministry, organized them into the denominational pattern, taught them a financial system and self-government and assuring them of counsel in case it was needed, passed on to new fields to raise up another such Church.

Unfortunately, there are other denominations that after fifty years have no such outlook. They seriously think that it is necessary for the mission to control the church, and by virtue of control of the lands on which some of their people "squat", or other control of their economy, they themselves are able to hold pastorates and they do not train and "ordain elders in every church." They may be sincere in the oft repeated dictum, "They are not ready for it yet," but one must also ask sincerely, "When would present methods develop them sufficiently for them to receive autonomy within the scope of the denomination?" Or is it an excuse; another colour bar, one practice for new American congregations and another for those of other races?

CHAPTER IX

Devolution – Changing from Mission to Church Support and Government

The crux of the economic problem of the missionary church can be expressed as follows:

> How can a relatively expensive institution, a product of an alien, high grade economy and living standards, be indigenized and financed in councils of lower economic standards when the bulk of the church members are drawn from the classes of the lowest economic levels?[13]

As this problem must be faced sooner or later by every mission that has not followed New Testament order, we would present some suggestions to be used in introducing negotiations aiming at devolution for the mission and indigenization for the Church.

Primarily, we must admit that however unsatisfactory a work may be in the matter of self-government, self-support and self-propagation, the present status has been brought about, not by the planning of the people, but by the methods we have introduced and followed. Granting this is the position, it would be idle to blame the clay for the form it has been given by the potter. Would it not then be better for us to admit our responsibility for the present condition of affairs, and plan a new form for the vessel that has been marred in our hands?

In explaining this to the congregation, we might further confess that in following our own methods, and those of men, we had not sought out the order of the Acts and Epistles, which were written for our instruction and guidance, nor yet had we studied the work of men who had followed these Scriptures. We now see that this is the cause of our failure to build a Church of the New Testament pattern, such as the Apostles planted, which was able to assume responsibility for

---

13. Likely from Davis, 1942

the evangelization of its people. "From you sounded forth the Word of the Lord not only in Macedonia and Achaia, but also in every place your faith to God-ward is spread abroad" (1 Thess 1:8).

Having thus accepted the responsibility for the unsatisfactory of our work, we could humbly propose to our people that we now desire to study, with them, the Scriptural plan. We are convinced that this is in the interests of the Church, for if it is to do its work, it must be self-contained.

We see that in the early church, as well as in early Methodism and other branches of the Church, every saved one bore witness to the truth. Most of the sermons preached were those of laymen who had their own living before they were saved, and devoted some time to church work freely. Some of these were ordained deacons and elders, and became "overseers" of the flock (Acts 20:28). This made the financial burden light for the church, and with tithes and offerings there was no lack.

As our system has not trained our people in giving, seeing we provided so much for them, and necessity was not laid upon them, we realize that it would be a hardship on the full-time workers were we to withdraw all mission support at once and make them dependent on the congregation. We also realize that the stipends were set by us and not by the churches, and may be higher than they are able to pay. We should talk these matters over with them, with the object of making the church strong and self-supporting, as were those of New Testament times.

They should understand that our carrying all these churches has been a steadily increasing burden on the Mission and unless some of them become self-supporting, the Mission will not be able to open new fields and so will not be able to "go into all the world", as the Master commanded. Indeed, these younger churches ought to be themselves opening new fields, as did the church of the Thessalonians, and others. Those who are saved should not give less for the Gospel than they did for the religion they followed before they were saved, and such contributions should support the New Testament order.

We propose, therefore, as a beginning, that the national conference (of which the missionaries are members), take control of, and assume responsibility for the support of their workers, and evolve some plan, including the tithe and offerings, whereby they may be able to do this. In order to expedite this plan the Mission will accord one year of grace for planning and adopt a plan of annual reductions of the stipends paid by it to national conference workers. It will also adopt the New Testament order of ordaining suitably-trained deacons and elders in the churches. We are sure that with the blessing of God and the earnest cooperation of all, we can see a better day wherein the churches will be able to use their full strength and enthusiasm in the work of God.

A Swedish Mission Does It

They had opened missions in remote parts of Congo and had a numerous following. It was impressed on them that they were not building a church with its roots in the ground under its feet and consequently it might, through the removal of the mission by war or otherwise, come to grief. They took council among themselves and the majority agreed that the church should have its own financial system and support its pastors. To accomplish this they decided, rather drastically, to withhold one-quarter of the mission's support at the end of each quarter and to expect the church provide for this, thus changing the venue of support from the mission to the church in a year. A senior missionary who had seen a great work built up, central in which was a mission-paid, African worker, feared the new regime, as he had responded to the pressure of this worker and raised his salary from time to time until he knew it to be beyond the financial ability of the church to pay. He feared that rather than take a cut and continue in the work to which he was called, he would go into commercial or Government service where he would receive much more than his present income. Without this worker he feared that he could not carry on and so his lifework would be ruined.

There was opposition to the new order, particularly in this place, but the church finally accepted the responsibility. Then a deputation waited on this man and told him that he knew he was living in sin. They said that as long as the white people were paying him, they would not report it as it would deprive him of his wages, but now that the church was to pay him they would not give the Lord's money to him unless he confessed. It was useless for him to pretend innocence to his African brethren for his manner of life could not be hidden from them, so he went to the missionary with his confession, and then to the church, to which it was no surprise. Others unburdened their hearts in confession and there broke out a revival such as had not been known. The missionary found that his life work, instead of ending had a new beginning.

Schisms

Towards the close of the last century, difficulties arose between certain missions and the African churches and their folds, which resulted in a breaking away from missionary leadership. The rift once made, speedily widened until there are reported to be now (1950), over six hundred of such separatist movements in the African sub-continent. As far back as 1926, a governmental commission was appointed in the Union of South Africa to enquire into the cause of these numerous schisms. Colonial governments, being overwhelmingly out-numbered by the people they rule, usually suffer from nerves whenever anything like a mass movement of any kind occurs. Their report traced several of the principal sects to their origin and states the following.

In many cases the unsympathetic attitude of the white missionaries is responsible for the breaking away of the native Minister and his adherents. They considered that if the white controllers of native churches had been more brotherly and patient and had displayed a greater anxiety to guide than to rule, the religious life of the natives would have been less troubled and unrest less universal.[14]

The Church may rightly feel that it has a duty to study the moral character of actions of government, but here the tables were turned, for it was the government that was asking the church to set its house in order on a moral issue.

It is noteworthy that where indigenous churches have considered themselves handicapped by missionary leadership, they have not been deterred from separation by the economic advantages they thereby relinquish, and that some of them have developed a sound program; notably the National Presbyterian Churches of Brazil.

"Anxiety to Guide"

Serious mistakes were made in colonial procedure in the early days when ignorance of the customs of the people, based in animism, provoked them to rebellion.[15] In South Africa, a disease, fatal to cattle, was caused by the bite of a tick. The government built dipping tanks and required that all cattle be put through a poison solution, periodically, to kill the ticks.

---

14. A.W. Roberts, *Report of the Native Churches Commission*, Cape Town: Union of South Africa, 1925.
15. The original manuscript attributes this statement to Edwin W. Smith, *The Golden Stool*. London: Holborn Publishing House, 1926.

This was done, but as the disease persisted it was found that the poison did not penetrate to all the ticks in the thick tuft of hair on the tails so an order was issued to shave these tufts. Immediately they objected. White men, some of them born in the country, whose understanding of both the people and their language, chiefly of the imperative mood, would have counseled force, which might have led to bloodshed. But men of good will sat down "tete-a-tete" and enquired why they were willing to dip their cattle but unwilling to shave the tails. The explanation brought out that they did not object to shaving the tails of most of the cows but only of particular ones. In ancestral worship, a cow occupies an important place. Brides cannot pray to the ancestors of their husbands but only to those of their fathers. When a bride goes to live with her husband she is given a cow by her father. When her children are sick, she plaits hairs from her cow's tail, puts it around her child's neck, prays to her father's ancestors and the child could get well. Now the government required that the tail be shaved and what would happen when the children got sick? The order was changed. Permission was given to hand dress the tails of these particular cows and not cut the hair, which did not lower the prestige of government, was equally effective and caused no trouble.

Tenants and Lands

Not having been instructed in the Christian pattern of inter-racial brotherhood, before going to the field, I readily accepted the current colonial pattern of economy as a necessity. If my conscience stood aghast at the spectacle of a people denied the right to buy land, in the country of their fathers, without franchise and reduced to a subsistence economy, I first endured, then pitied and then embraced, for the mission pattern differed in that on its mission farms, where a higher moral standard of living was required of its tenants, and eviction was the only recourse a missionary in charge of tenants had, his heart ached when he was forced to take action, for the church could not sponsor slums. Holding lands and tenants had become an entanglement. To escape from this, one group of tenants were permitted to buy the mission lands on which they resided and they have gladly paid the purchase price in full.

CHAPTER X

When Harvest Comes

Discernment of Spirits Essential

Quite apart from missionary leadership, there have been mass movements in Africa, involving scores of thousands of people. Their origin cannot always be traced for "the wind bloweth were it listeth." Like all religious mass movements, they break over the accepted pattern in many ways and sweep into their orbit a "mixed multitude" with many practices decidedly unorthodox, with characteristics definitely African.

To the missionary from the West, these movements, entirely beyond his control, can be aggravating if not terrifying. He may never have seen anything but profound decorum in church services, or if he has seen expressions of emotion in which the worshipper has shouted for joy, ran or danced before the Lord, the demonstrations he now encounters are those of another people with a different social order, with ways, centuries old, of expressing their inward emotions in social behaviour. It is all so new and so perplexing. He does not understand it. He is afraid of it and tries to suppress it. But they move, en masse, and cannot be bottled up in our Western order, so trouble looms. They believe they are led of God, and we would be prepared to grant that were it not that there is so much in the movement that seems foreign to the Gospel.

These "prophet movements", led by an African, have turned thousands from their fetishes and from many of their sins. They usually bore testimony to a change of heart and to a joy in the Lord. They loved syncopated singing and accompanied it with a rhythm of the body, all in unison, men in a group in close formation, each separately. Women acted similarly in entirely separated groups. In one such group, deaths were reported from holding the person under water in baptism. They expected them to rise from the dead. In such cases the government must necessarily, and did intervene. But not all extravagances took this form. There was a case, well-remembered, that happened long ago where the missionaries in distress appealed to the government. They, in an effort to enforce obedience, passed the death sentence on some of the leaders. The missionaries interceded for them and sentence was changed to banishment to remote parts of the country among strange tribes. Years later, when missionaries penetrated into these areas, they reported finding large Christian communities that had built for themselves places of worship and were preaching the Gospel. The missions went on with their work after these disturbers were removed but they are not sure that the matter was handled discreetly and they freely admit that the pillars in their churches, on whom they have depended all these years, were among those who came out in that movement.

In the *Congo Mission News*, Dr. A.C. Stanley Smith of the Church Missionary Society, reports on a movement of the Holy Spirit that has caused concern to many, under the heading of "Revival."

Revival

For the last fifteen years there has been a movement of the Spirit of God in Revival in these parts of East Africa, not confined to any one mission. Without any organization, it has spread far and wide – in parts of Eastern Congo, in Uganda, Tanganyika Territory, Kenya and the Sudan. It is beginning to be seen even in England and on the Continent. The people are becoming known as the BALOKOLE, (the saved ones). Many missions with tragic experiences of separatist movements, have heard of this movement with anxiety and even suspicion. But this attitude is steadily giving way to appreciation and to thankfulness to God. For as the years have passed, it is becoming more and more clear that it is the working of the Holy Spirit. Mistakes and blemishes there have been of course. It could not be otherwise with human agents; there have been failures. But the marks of the Lord Jesus are so manifest that fears are being allayed and missionaries are rejoicing in the evidences of God's power.

The basic feature in it all is conviction of sin and perhaps, most searching of all, sin in the believer. Following on this conviction, goes the testimony of cleansing through the blood of Jesus, and the possibility of real victory. There is a warmth of fellowship, a joy, a peace and a quiet humility among these people. Far from being a separatist movement, it discourages any breaking away and I do not hesitate to say that it is the biggest influence in our part of Africa today for drawing together white and black.

In our work there are now well over 10,000

baptised Christians; and as regards the ministry, four new deacons have been ordained, making the total of our ordained ministry eight. Some indications of the spiritual progress of the Church may be found in their giving. Of our seven stations, three are fully self-supporting. The total amount given by the Church for the support of their pastors and evangelists, the building of their churches, and the maintenance of the work, came to 1,137,101 francs.

As we look on our own work on the one hand, often so hard-going and apparently fruitless, and then we see the majestic sweep of the power of God in human lives, we take courage, and go into 1950 with the assurance that though practical difficulties seem to mount up increasingly before us, the Lord will see us through (The above report is for 1949. At 43 francs to the dollar it represents $26,444.00).[16]

CHAPTER XI

Building the Spiritual Church

Experiences in Mozambique

Missionary work in Mozambique was in its infancy when we arrived there in 1902 and, the African Church, although there in embryo as a little flock of believers, had scarcely recognized itself nor been recognized by the missionaries. Thousands of Africans were going as labourers to the rapidly developing gold mines of the Transvaal, and as our society and others opened work there and taught the converts to read in night schools, a man came back from time to time who

---

16. long quotation from *Congo Mission Now*

was aflame with a desire to teach his people the way of salvation. This made the prospects of evangelizing the vast areas hopeful.

Cheered by helpers from this unexpected quarter, the missionaries set to work with enthusiasm. It probably never occurred to them that the "little flock" they saw growing around them was the Church, a living organism they were to develop and train, and upon which would fall the right as well as the responsibility of evangelizing their people. This lack of comprehension may have been responsible for the years of heart-searching that followed, for with growth in numbers and responsibility the church grew in self-consciousness, and the urge within it to enter into provinces that had been exclusively that of the mission was not always understood and was resented. But, as the Gospel plan seems to be that they must increase and we must decrease, the process could not be held in check indefinitely. It was only when its rights were recognized and ungrudgingly given to it that a new day dawned for both Church and mission.

The plan adopted by the mission was to offer a scholarship, preachership or stationship to an individual, a Sunday School or a Church to support; self-support having never been considered as a practical possibility. There was an immediate response, and outschools were opened far and near. But weak links soon began to appear. The system was based on a supply of foreign money, and, although there were thousands of people waiting for the Gospel and numbers of men anxious to be sent to teach them, the work could not go forward without ever-increasing sums of money from overseas. It all seemed so foreign to the New Testament way. Offerings were taken, but as there was no necessity for them to give, they let the mission provide the money, and they received no practical training in supporting the Lord's work. Workers naturally pressed for higher wages, although their stipends made them the envy of their people, and so far from developing the grace of supporting their pastors, they begged from them. The pastors, being financially independent of their membership tended to assume the attitude of a chief rather than of a pastor, an attitude to which the human heart seems prone. The mission built their houses and schools, provided blankets and clothing for their children and a grinding mill for the village. It happened that when these pastors were called for a refresher course, they considered gold digging more important. When some concession had been obtained, they were anxious to return home and our purpose was foiled. We began to wonder if there was one who "would shut the doors *for naught?*" (Mal 1:10).

It was not that there was nothing in these men that could be appealed to beside love of earthly things. They were of the same clay as others who returned to their homes in remote areas and began to work for God. They gathered their sustenance from the soil under their feet the same as their people did. But they knew how to draw spiritual bread from the heaven over their heads; a new thing there. They spent no more time in teaching than their brethren did in being taught, and as the epistle instructs, "Let him that is taught in the word communicate to him that teacheth in all good things" (Gal 6:6). They were eligible to receive little gifts of food, to be helped in their cultivation and in other love-inspired ways, known to the African, so that support of the pastor and of the Church was incidental with the coming of the Gospel. It was only when numbers had turned to God and needed baptism that they sought out some distant missionary, and then it was not for money.

An urgent appeal came to me from such an indigenous group. I walked several days to get to them. Their leader came two days to meet me and escorted me to his home. We sat down together and he told me what things God had done for them. He gathered the people and told them the Good News. Then they came and built a little house where they could gather and be taught, to sing and to pray. He had brought a few wall, reading charts, a precious asset, and was teaching them to read the Scriptures. Many had been saved and had moved their huts to his village, for by leaving the kraals of their people, they were free from ancestral worship and were in a Christian influence. I ate and slept in his house and spoke to them the Word of Life, thus confirming to them what he had taught. He showed me a large group that he considered ready for baptism. I examined them and then, on inquiry, ascertained that there was a lake about two miles away where they could be baptized in water as they requested. It was infested with crocodiles but they said the Lord would surely protect them while doing what He commanded. So, in their faith, I went in and baptized sixty. I never visited them again for I left that field. I fain would have given their God-called leader authority to gather them around the table of the Lord and to baptize but that was "above my might."

 To preach the Gospel, one surely needs all the training one can acquire, year by year, but to baptize or to administer communion seems such a simple thing that ability to read the service could suffice; and yet we send unlearned men to preach and deny them the right to serve their people in the matter of these sacred but simple ordinances. Our Lord sent His disciples to do both.

 Our people were not inferior to these in their love and devotion to their Lord. The fruit that seemed so bitter to us was produced by our system. Because we paid every preacher sent out, no one could be expected to go without our paying them, nor would those under appointment be willing to see others go out unless they were so paid. It would be equivalent to sending one's self. The system seemed to be such a negation of the spirit of the New Testament, and the possibilities of building a New Testament Church, with this system seemed so remote, that with a determined effort, much difficulty and heart-searching, the system was changed and a Church has grown up with a burden for souls, not only at home but in the regions beyond. It now supports its pastors and sends missionaries. After a similar change of system in South Africa our African leaders asked, "Why did you not teach this from the beginning?" Indeed, why not?

Experiences in Ruanda-Urundi

When the call came to open a new field, our aim was to build a church that was self-supporting from the beginning, and thus escape the trying experiences of devolution, trying for both the church and the mission. I knew there were such churches in most, if not all, major mission lands, and that an influential group published a magazine and other literature on the subject, but had not known how any such church had been started from the beginning.

    I expected to have some time to study procedure after seeing the people from among whom the Lord would call out His Church, but scarcely had two days passed before I had the issue thrust upon me by a group of men coming to work, asking for a school. It was a test indeed. Should I build a school for them, and after some of them were saved, try to get them into self-support, or should I begin now? Would it rebuff them were I to ask them to build? To wait till some future time made a strong appeal, especially as it would obviate the necessity of making a decision and of formulating a definite plan then. It seemed so easy to let the mission carry the financial burden until some future time, ignoring the fact that the group might be willing and able to assume the responsibility if shown the way. My experience had been that the paid agents of the mission sought higher wages and further concessions, until their remuneration was so far above that of their people that the Church would not, perhaps could not, undertake the burden. It was in the interest of the young church that this should not be allowed to happen. When the mission thought that the time had come for the church to take over the paid agents, they were not in favor of what appeared to be a loss of income and prestige, and the church was not pleased to assume a financial burden heretofore carried for them. In such a case, it would be difficult indeed to effect the change and this crisis would not come to a people who are willing to be taught, and that, if unsatisfactory results come from our teaching methods, we should not blame them.

I had been much in prayer for guidance and was impressed that I should begin at the beginning in what seemed to be the right way, so I told them that I also wanted a school, but if we were to have a school, we must have a building. They assented. I then explained to them that I would pay them to build for me houses in which I would eat or sleep or store my goods, but in the case of a school building, I would only enter to teach them, and so I would not pay them to build it. What was my surprise and joy to hear their immediate response that they would call the people to come to work for God, and they would build it. I had a feeling of having been on the brink of a chasm and of having almost fallen into it.

Not wishing to discourage them or to penalize the little group of today for the larger group expected in the future, I laid out a small building 10 x 15 feet. I gave them some posts, for I wanted the mission to have some part in this first little token building and they called men, women and children to come to work for God. They responded with alacrity and joy, and in an afternoon, the poor, little structure was completed, and all entered for the initial, dedicatory service. One end was altogether open for light. There were no windows, seats nor doors, and yet they had the great joy and satisfaction of having wrought for God, and doubtless, in that act most of them made their decision to give themselves to Him. Certain it was that the fierce persecution that followed did not deter them from persevering or others from coming to work for God. The little building was soon too small, and they enlarged it. Again it was too small and they put a cross section on it. When that would no longer accommodate the congregation, we moved to another site and built on a larger scale, 20 x 60 feet, with a transept extending fifteen feet on either side. This was enlarged twice, always by the mission giving the poles and the people working for God. The enthusiasm of the groups of from 250 to 300 people working for God was a joy to behold. One received the impression that when they became a spiritual church it would surely be a working church.

Two months after I had located at Muyebe, alone, my wife and two daughters joined me. Crowds were pressing on us for medicines and to learn. While my wife was busy trying to make a home for us in our four-roomed mud floor house, with calico for windows, and trying to gather and cook food for us without a stove, our elder daughter took over the school. She had to make wall charts and use any scrap of board she could get to make blackboards. Our younger daughter took over the crowds that came every morning for medicines. To prevent them from thronging her, we erected a small shelter from the sun and rain through which they had to pass in line. Around this she planted seeds, and, when a canopy of vines and flowers covered it, visitors named it "The Morning Glory Clinic".

By the time that some of the Barundi[17] were saved and had learned to read, there were calls from different places for schools. A site would be secured from the Authorities, and on a set day the whole congregation would leave off work to go

---

17. In the native language, Kirundi, the word *Barundi* means Burundians or the people of Burundi.

and work for God, and, with the help of the local people, they usually finished the building in a day or two.

I had told the Barundi that the mission would open mission stations here and there and carry on the usual program, but that the African church would have to carry the Gospel to their people; "from you sounded out the word of the Lord" (1 Thess 1:8), so when teachers began to go out, the manner of their support called for consideration. I pointed out that it was unfair for them to work for the mission and receive pay and then send out their representatives without pay, and if they would deal justly they must give an offering. They said, "An offering is good; we want an offering." Asked what they could give, they said a man could give a franc a month; a woman or big girl or boy, fifty centimes; and the children, from ten to thirty centimes. This I considered generous, considering their income, and approximately a tenth. It was explained that although they were all enrolled in our school register, and when saved and considered worthy, they would be baptised, we would now begin a new register of those who wished to bind themselves together for the purpose of taking the Gospel to their people and who were willing to pay this offering. Their being enrolled was purely voluntary, and paying this offering would not insure their baptism. They all asked to be enrolled.

As we were training an embryo church and it was important that they should learn to give and handle church funds, I bought an iron box with a padlock and two keys. The offerings went into this box, together with a cash book. A key was given to each of two stewards, chosen by themselves, and the box was to remain, for safe-keeping, at the mission. They were hesitant to accept the keys, fearing suspicion; but as it was explained that I could not take the money because I had no key, and they could not take it because they had the box in their possession only as they carried it to meeting in the presence of the congregation, they accepted office. They take the box to the meetings and open it in the presence of the congregation, enter the amount of the offering, lock it and bring it back. The missionary makes out a pay sheet for two or three months, showing the amount each preacher-teacher is to be paid. They are given this, and at the end of each month they make the payments. They were told that under no circumstances would the mission put money into their box. The mission would bring missionaries and do the training, but the Church must take the Gospel to the people. Payment in full is contingent on there being enough money in the box. Each adherent and member has a ticket on which his monthly offering is entered, and the African pastor has a book in which these records are kept. Tithing is taught and urged, not so much by the missionaries, who all tithe and use it in other ways, but by the Barundi themselves. When they began to give, they asked that the missionaries help them by giving five francs monthly. We agreed to this but stipulated that ours be kept in a small box inside the big one and used, not to support the preacher-teachers, but as a home mission fund, in their power but to be used to buy trees et cetera, to build in new places.

When calls came for African missionaries to go to open work in distant places, those who were called of God and sent used the same methods among the people to whom they came, but in order to provide for travel and initial expenses, the Church provided another box called, "Let us go on" (Heb 6:1). Into this box, they put monthly, a tithe of all money received in the boxes on the circuits. An African preacher and a layman have been entrusted with the keys, and the quarterly conference controls disbursements.

The great joy and enthusiasm of the young church is a pleasure to see. They have been endued with power from on high, and no self-denial is too great. The wives, as well as their husbands, are ready to answer God's call. Progress was slow in the beginning, but after twelve years, on the strength of the African Church and the blessing of God, 95 out-stations have been established and 107 preacher-teachers sent out. A precious harvest of 1,508 have been baptized, 1,423 have been received on probation, and there are 11,379 in the schools. Three preachers have been ordained Deacon. We give to God all the praise for what He has wrought through the efforts of each and every missionary and the tiring efforts of our African brethren.

Circuit Plan – A Vehicle of a Forward Movement

Advance, so ardently desired, is not to be obtained by a system of revivals, as results show. There must be an every-member evangelism wherein each brings into the congregation the sheep he has sought with labor, prayers and tears. He may have already led them to the Lord or he may have brought them under the sound of the Gospel. He may have sought them in the workshop, in their homes or by the wayside. They will have to be sought and it is the duty of everyone to seek. The reward is sure. "Shall doubtless come again … bringing his sheaves" (Ps 126:6). Many have thanked God for that "shall doubtless'. Remind the Lord that He hath promised and keep right on sowing and seeking. He shall doubtless return bringing his sheaves; to the Sunday School, to the church and to the Lord. When individual effort on the part of all the members of the church has brought in new faces, it is time, not for revival, for such a working church does not need reviving, but for special effort.

If each church in centers of population could expand itself into the circuit of former Methodism, there would be a doubling or multiplication of membership. The human means of accomplishing this is already in our hands – our loyal, enthusiastic youth, waiting to be sent out into the highways and hedges under church direction. To accomplish this, in Africa, recourse is had to the Circuit Plan, a simple device whereby many of the laity are sent to various places, singly or by twos or groups, if they enlist their friends, under the direction of the pastor. This PLAN that directs certain lay members of the Y.P.M.S.[18] or others to a certain place at a certain time, focuses and directs, under the hand of the pastor or leader of the group, the efforts of these lay people, young and old, to the church of tomorrow, with all their talent and enthusiasm. They would not be sent to distant places but to their own city for which they have a special responsibility. An open-air at a certain place could be an assignment on the Plan. The visitation of a block of houses or street could be another. To sing and pray with a number of sick people could be another. To gather children into a home for Sunday School could be another, or to organize a prayer meeting in a home where it might be welcomed.

The Plan lists and numbers the names of any and all who are to be used in this way. It would cover a month or a quarter, as a calendar. The places where the service is to be rendered are listed. A number under a date, at a place, indicates who is to go, when and where.

Where there is a family or two and no pastor, make it a point of the nearest circuit and give them a plan that will set them definitely to work. Let them hold a weekly prayer meeting and invite their friends. Occasionally send one of the young people to help them. Have them seek for children from house-to-house and start a Sunday School. Five or six would make a good start. Send a team of your young people to help. One could be Superintendent. With importunate prayer and effort, it will take root for the Word of God says, "He … shall

---

18. Young People's Missionary Society

doubtless come again with rejoicing, bringing his sheaves" (Ps 126:6).

When Rev. Ernest Cooper was pastor of the West Avenue Church in Hamilton, the needs of a new area in the city was on his heart. He took a group of his people there on Sunday afternoons for an open-air Sunday School. They sang and fourteen young people gathered. They taught, distributed literature and announced Sunday School for the next Sunday. Twenty-eight came and numbers continued to increase. The coming of autumn necessitated a building but their Father knew what things they had need of. They were attracted to a small hall, owned by the Police, but they could not get the use of it. Then it changed hands, the organization of Scouts securing it. They readily allowed it to be used for Sunday School. The children took envelopes and brought money. In the Spring, they built a hall of their own. Now the place supports a pastor and Church program. The Sunday School is limited in numbers by the size of the hall only. Perhaps it is now a case of arrested development, which should not happen for it should enlarge its borders and hive off in turn. An indication to them that God's approbation was upon the project from the beginning was, that during the summer months, it never rained during the Sunday School hour, and during the erection of the hall, in April and May, when rain would have ruined the paper board sheeting, it never rained until it was safely covered and then it almost poured down. Of the first fourteen, one was called to prepare for the ministry and one as a missionary to India.

Editor's Note: *Haley's manuscript ends at this point. It would seem that he was in the process of illustrating his principles with concrete examples before moving to a summative conclusion. The following article by Haley was the substance of his address to the Annual Convention of the Evangelical*

Fellowship of Mission Agencies (EFMA) in 1949. It represents a succinct summary of Haley's thesis in the uncompleted, unpublished manuscript.[19]

The Indigenous Church: The Biblical Method of Missions

Building the Indigenous Church in Mid-Africa

J.W. Haley

The "indigenous" church works in Africa.

By indigenous I mean a Christian church which is native to its location in race, language and custom – not exotic, foreign or imported. In Africa – a church of Africans for Africans and which Africans support.

This type of mission work is being discussed so widely that it may seem to be brand new. Far from that, it is almost contradiction of terms for we may well ask if groups of believers are churches at all if not indigenous.

The churches founded by the Apostles were indigenous but "modern methods" produce, too often, poor "hot-house" results that cannot be compared with those stalwart,

---

19. The article is the presentation that John Wesley Haley gave on April 20, 1949 to the Evangelical Fellowship of Mission Agencies (EFMA) Annual Convention in Chicago. Originally published in the *United Evangelical Action* (UEA) on August 15, 1949 (and later as a pamphlet, with two other presentations, which included this summary comment: "These three messages given at the EFMA Annual Convention in Chicago are reprinted from UEA. The three speakers represent Africa, Latin America, and Asia. The increase of nationalism throughout the world demands an understanding of this method.") The article is reprinted here with the permission of the EFMA, now part of MissioNexus (www.missionexus.org).

aggressive congregations from which "sounded out the word of the Lord not only in Macedonia and Ashaia, but also in every place" (I Thess. 1:8). When we re-discover the New Testament methods they seem new.

Under customary methods a mission may be well established and have a great number of paid agents over a wide area, and a numerous baptized following, but may not constitute a church. Business concerns like Lever Brothers have large interests, such as plantations and stores, in Africa. In order to carry on their business they must have a great number of Africans trained for many and various occupations. If they are saved from sin they are more faithful stewards. To meet this need such companies have opened schools and employed religious and secular teachers thus doing a tremendous amount of good and probably leading many to a knowledge of the Lord but these are not the shareholders or directors of the company but only its servants. This is no doubt "good business" but the aims of a mission should be vastly different from these. Our aim is to bring all Africans into "The Company" and, if we follow Apostolic example, with all the expedition possible. It may be easy for us to tell ourselves, "They are not ready for it yet," but who other than the Holy Spirit can decide that, and His plan is revealed in the Acts and Epistles.

The constantly increasing number of pagans in the world warns us that Christian Missions are failing, notwithstanding all our money, men and modern methods. Perhaps, in looking for the reason, we should consider the difference between "servants of the mission" and "servants of Christ." Unless we missionaries can build believers into the Church of Christ and so bring out their full force, their full love, their full devotion and full loyalty to Him, and then push them ahead in the task of evangelism, while we train their leaders and continue to decrease while they increase, the task will not be done.

I began in Africa with "modern methods" over forty years ago. We aimed, uncertainly, at a self-supporting church, but with no definite method of bringing it into existence. We paid the preacher-teachers and gave them money to build their homes, schools and for many other things. Numbers increased rapidly and a true work of soul saving was accomplished. These leaders considered us to be "rich" and begged from us on all occasions. They themselves became the "well-to-do" and their people, instead of learning to support their pastors, begged from them. It was all too evident that this system would never build an indigenous church and, cost what it would, would have to be changed.

I could not blame these African Christians if they were mercenary for they were the product of our own system. We had followed our Guide. With patience, humility and love, on both sides, and a study of the methods of the Apostles, the change was accomplished without loss and a Church, the Church of Jesus Christ, took its God-appointed place.

Not only do they now support their own work but they send out African missionaries. It is an inspiring thing to see them coming together to their annual gathering, some of them walking as much as two and three hundred miles. Interest does not flag whether they are discussing business, preaching the Gospel or witnessing in the great congregation. The great day is the one when African missionaries thrill the vast concourse with the triumphs of the grace of God as they extend the fighting line. Then all have a part as they crowd their way to the tables to lay their offerings of cash and kind before the Lord that their workers may go out and the good work go on. A new day has dawned.

Indigenous from the Beginning

When I went into Central Africa I was tempted to wait

until we had a congregation of saved people before planning self-support. By then I had found that the leaders did not want to be thrown on congregations untrained by necessity in giving, which would mean demotion, nor did the people want to support their leaders. Why should they? The mission was "rich." All were united against the plan. Quite evidently the beginning was the place to begin, but how? I thought I would have six months to consider but the third day after I came to an untouched area the people asked for a school and the whole proposition in a nutshell, had to be faced.

I lifted up my heart in prayer and with great fear told them that I was paying them to help me to build houses where I would eat or sleep or store my goods but a school building was for none of these. It was God's. I would not use it at all but only go into it to teach them and so I would not pay them to build it. What was my surprise and joy when they replied without hesitation that they would call the people to "work for God," and they would build it. It was one of the great surprises of my life. I had the feeling of having been on the brink of a chasm, and of having almost fallen into it. They appointed a day and as I wanted to have a part in the work of this little, embryo church I gave them the posts to stand in the ground and we built a place about 12 x15 feet. Purposely it was small for I wanted them to be able to finish it in a day and I did not want to penalize the first few for the increased numbers expected later.

They called the people and away they went, men, women and children, all over the place to bring in grass, cords and reeds. You would have thought that they had known me as a friend for years. The call to "work for God" appealed to them and they brought the grass and set the posts and built the place, with one end open to let in the light, in a few hours, and a happier group I never saw. After a time other communities wanted schools. They wanted to work for God too. After permission to occupy a site had been secured from the Belgian Authorities the original group would go on to help the new community to build.

Building schools in various places raised the question of supporting the preacher-teachers who went out. We told them that we would open missions here and there and teach many things but we would not be responsible for these "out schools." They received the Gospel freely at the mission and must take it to their own people. They said they would do it if we taught them how. We told them it would be necessary for them to make an offering and to this they agreed. When asked how much they could give they named a small, monthly offering, differing for men, women, and for children. They have since accepted the tithe as the standard.

At first all were enrolled on the school register but now I proposed that I would make out a new register for those who wanted to form a company whose purpose was the evangelizing of the surrounding territory. I stressed that I would not hasten their baptism (a thing they greatly desired) nor need they join if they did not wish to. I expected a few of the men would join but what was my amazement when, all – men, women and children – asked to be enrolled. I would never have thought of taxing children, but children are in the Kingdom of God, and I was wrong, as I so often am, but they were right. Some of our very best givers were some of these same little children. I remember a little chap about eight years of age coming up so proudly with two little coins of about a mill value each saying, "Next month I will bring three." He went without clothing most of the day but he was a staunch supporter of the church. Often little boys and girls asked me for work to get their church money, and they usually got it. My business was to build a church and these were the best material.

After twelve years there were over one hundred African

workers out in the districts all supported by the African church. Three thousand have been baptized or are in preparation for baptism and fifteen thousand have been enrolled in our schools. The gifts of the Holy Spirit have been given to many and, recognizing this, three have been ordained as Deacons and others are in training. The Lord, through the power of the Holy Spirit has wrought all this through His called ones.

We are building a church – an indigenous church – for today and for all time. We firmly believe it is the Lord's way.

Appendix

Editor's comment: *In his uncompleted manuscript, Haley had included a stand-alone section, perhaps an appendix, about the unique inter-church/agency environment in Ruanda-Urundi, in which he played an influential role. This section of his manuscript is included here.*

Advisory United Church Council

The Alliance of Protestant Missions in Ruanda-Urundi

The group of missionaries the Lord sent into Ruanda-Urundi came from Britain, Denmark, Sweden and America. They held in common the necessity of the new birth. They realized that to propagate denominationalism would divide religiously those they found united politically under their chiefs and kings. Those who desired to form an Alliance came from different denominations, Anglicans, Baptists, Pentecostals, Free Methodists, Friends and National Holiness Society. As they were supported by different groups, they were under the necessity of maintaining their identity. However, as each was there to build the Church of Christ they had this motive in common and could build their several divisions into one army, if they so desired. Each group kept their Board fully informed in the matter but did not ask for formal denominational approval of church union as that would involve delay and difficulties that might be found to be indissolvable. Unity without uniformity was their aim and this is a spiritual quality rather than organic union.

To promote spiritual unity a three-day convention of missionaries was called at a Baptist mission. As they were seeking unity among themselves and the prevention of division of spirit among the Africans, the Lord who prayed, on the eve of His suffering, "That they all may be one," (John 17:21) was very present in definite approbation, and all felt that such convention must be held from time to time. Messages from the Lord were brought by different speakers and time was taken for united prayer. A simple constitution was drawn up which set out what was proposed, namely, the formation of an Alliance of Protestant Missions that desired the building of a spiritual, united, African Church.

When the African churches learned of the great blessing their missionaries had received, they immediately asked for such conventions. These were arranged, at first at missions and later on hill tops in groves. Had not their Master gone up into a mountain where multitudes came unto Him and remained for three days? The local people built a few booths of sticks and grass for the workers from a distance. The others slept in the open. They came with their food, for to supply food would mean the discontinuance of such meetings, but the local people did augment it freely. Missionaries attending brought tents and provided for themselves. An effort was made to keep the numbers below two thousand.

Africans wake early so the day began at dawn, with prayer all over the hill. Then they formed themselves into groups of men, women, boys, and girls with older Christians in each group. Joyful singing of hymns began all over the hill followed by confession of sin by the burdened ones in each group. Then they knelt to ask forgiveness claiming the promise that "If we confess our sins, he is faithful and just to forgive us *our* sins" (1 John 1:9). Then they arose and praised God for deliverance. At appointed times, all came together for two great meetings daily that lasted about three hours each, in which there was prayer, singing, two or three sermons, testimonies of deliverance from many and terrible sins; "the contrite sinner's voice, returning from his ways."[20]

Previous to these conventions, denominationalism was taking hold. The African Episcopalians had not known that there were Christian groups in the world other than themselves and the Roman Catholics. They were greatly confused, and especially so, when they encountered the Friends from Kansas. "But you are not Christians: How could you be? You are not even baptized", they said. But after the fellowship of the conventions, a sense of spiritual unity came and they said, "We do not understand your teaching but we do know that you are the Lord's people and hereafter, when we travel through your part of the country, we are going to visit you for we are one in the Lord."

Spiritual unity having been obtained in this way, it was necessary that they have a council that would promote unity and take care of causes of division that would be sure to arise so the Alliance created the Advisory United Church Council. There was no united church, other than in the realm of the spirit, so it could only be an advisory council. It was composed of the missionaries who composed the Executive Committee of the Alliance, plus African representatives of the Alliance missions. There was a joint Presidency and joint Secretariat; an African and a missionary for each office. The

---

20. from James Montgomery's hymn, "Prayer is the Soul's Sincere Desire," 1818.

writer considers it to be the highest honor he has received that he was chosen to serve as the first joint President of this significant body, together with an African, and Episcopalian Minister. The Swedish Pentecostals were not free to join the Alliance, so their congregations were not represented on the Advisory United Church Council, but a warm fellowship existed and it was hoped that they too would receive permission to join.

The Council soon developed a sense of solidarity and responsibility and worked for uniformity in the training of the African clergy, the wages the Church should pay its preacher-teachers and other matters of common interest, wherein the different practices of different missions might tend to divide the Church as a whole. They showed remarkably sound sense in many ways. African chiefs with their councils have always ruled their people, heard causes and made war and peace, so in councils they are at their best. When there was a widespread demand all over the country for increases in the pay of church workers, the Council only allowed increases for the lowest paid men, and declined to vote salary increases for themselves, as they felt it would be too great a burden for the African Church. Their decisions were loyally accepted by all the Africans in all of the missions. No attempt was made to deal with differences in doctrine. Following the constitution of the United Church of South India, it was felt that if organic union was ever accomplished, denominational differences in the uniting groups should be respected for thirty years of united action, and then if changes were desired, the young Church itself should make them.

Missions in Congo, generally, have agreed to build *l'Eglise du Christ au Congo* (The Church of Christ in Congo), rather than to allow denominational pride to insist on dividing the African church after our unfortunate divisions. Church letters given by any mission are accepted by other missions, the same as their own. There is a sense of unity in that all are of the Church of Christ. They are being prepared for the day when they should manage and finance their own work and when the missionaries will assist and serve. Our Lord said, "I am among you as he that serveth", and the servant is not greater than his Lord.

The Church of Christ in Congo is rapidly coming to self-consciousness. Its first regional conference met in Blukwa (A.I.M.)[21] last year (1949). There were 72 Congolese delegates from 40 different mission stations and representing 21 different tribes. These, together with 14 missionary delegates, came from five Protestant missionary societies working in Ulele and Ituri districts. The Secretary of the Congo Protestant Council attended. His Spirit guided messages and helpful advice regarding the development of the Congo Church were greatly blessed to Africans and missionaries alike.

The Congolese wanted to know the reasons for the different methods of different missions and repeatedly drew them back to the New Testament. It was felt that there is a greater unity in our African Church than there is often in our homelands. Their clear cut and sane thinking sometimes found the solution to a problem before the missionaries could find the solution.

> We found that instead of considering the African Church leaders as mere children needing the guidance of missionary parents, the time has come to consider them rather as brethren as they lead the Church in Congo under the guidance of the Holy Spirit. It was quite evident also that our native leaders frequently show greater understanding than the missionary, when dealing with the many

21. Africa Inland Mission

problems peculiar to the African Church (from the secretarial report of the conference).

God is calling out His church here in Congo, and we came to realize in a new way that this Church is the CHURCH OF CHRIST IN CONGO rather than a number of units of the denominational groups from which we have come in our various home lands *(from the secretarial report of the conference)*.

3

The Indigenous Church in Burundi

Deogratias Nshimiyimana, Evariste Harerimana, Desire Mpfubusa

Déogratias Nshimiyimana [1]

Evariste Harerimana [2]

Désiré Mpfubusa [3]

INTRODUCTION

At the last General Conference in June of 2014, it was a privilege and an honor for me to be elected as the Bishop of the indigenous Free Methodist Church of Burundi. As long as I have been active in the Free Methodist Church of Burundi, I have known about John Wesley Haley and the building of the indigenous Free Methodist Church of Burundi. I have also known that the indigenous Church of Burundi is self-supporting, self-propagating and self-governing.

Right from the 1935 beginning at Muyebe, John Wesley Haley began building an indigenous church that would be

---

1. Rev. Déogratias Nshimiyimana is the current Bishop of the Free Methodist Church of Burundi and senior author of this part of the book.
2. Rev. Evariste Harerimana is the current Superintendent of the Rutunga District of the Western Conference of the Free Methodist Church of Burundi and served as a Research Assistant in the preparation of this part of the book.
3. Rev. Désiré Mpfubusa is a current pastor in the Western Conference of the Free Methodist Church of Burundi and served as a Research Assistant in the preparation of this part of the book.

self-supporting, self-propagating and self-governing. As an indigenous organization, the Church has supported itself, expanded itself and governed itself throughout its first 80 years in Burundi. The Church has continued and grown even through the difficult colonial times under the Belgians; 1914 to independence in 1962. The Burundi Church also stood firm during a series of civil wars in 1965, 1972, 1988 and, the longest and most devastating one, 1993 to 2005.

At Muyebe in 1961, the Church celebrated its 25 year anniversary, the establishment of full conference status and the ordination of the first African elders. At Muyebe in 1985, the Church celebrated the first 50 years and the installation of the first Burundian bishop, Rev. Noah Nzeyimana (1985-2000). Since then, there have been many important members, pastors and superintendents who have greatly contributed to the building and maintaining of the indigenous Church, including a series of indigenous bishops; Rev. Elie Buconyori (2000-2013), Rev. Onésphore Nzigo (2013-2014) and, now me, Rev. Déogratias Nshimiyimana (2014-).

In 1935, Haley had a vision of building an indigenous church in Burundi. The indigenous Free Methodist Church of Burundi now has a membership of 155,207 and 948 local churches.[4] In addition, the Church has many primary and secondary schools, a Bible school, a university, dispensaries, health clinics and two hospitals.

Haley's vision was larger than just Burundi. As the work took root in Burundi, Haley contributed to building indigenous Free Methodist Churches in Rwanda and what is

---

4. These figures are based on the most recent statistical information compiled by the districts and summarized by the conferences. According to the Free Methodist Church USA website, the Free Methodist Church of Rwanda currently has 111,514 members and 643 churches. See Free Methodist Church USA, "World Areas: Africa." http://fmcusa.org/fmwm/world-areas/africa/. May 30, 2015.

now known as the Democratic Republic of Congo.[5] Currently, more indigenous Free Methodist Churches are being developed in Kenya and Tanzania.

I A SELF-SUPPORTING INDIGENOUS ORGANIZATION

Haley wanted to build an indigenous church; a self-supporting indigenous church. The Free Methodist Church of Burundi is self-supporting.

The Free Methodist Church of Burundi raises funds at the local church level and the funds are managed at the local church level, the parish level, the district level, the annual conference level and, finally, the general conference level. *The Book of Discipline* for the Free Methodist Church of Burundi[6] supports the principle of a self-supporting indigenous church by requiring members to accept the personal responsibility for tithes and offering. The membership covenants state that every member has the responsibility to support the church and its work.

Domestic Funds

Almost all of the money within the self-supporting Free Methodist Church of Burundi is raised at the local level, that is, the local churches. At the local church level, both in the rural and urban areas, members are expected to tithe regularly

---

5. According to the Free Methodist Church USA website, the Free Methodist Church of the Democratic Republic of Congo currently has 160,000 members and 450 churches. See Free Methodist Church USA, "World Areas: Africa." http://fmcusa.org/fmwm/world-areas/africa/. May 30, 2015.
6. *The Book of Discipline* serves as the constitution or law for the Church and includes the denominational requirements and governing principles. Since *The Book of Discipline 2000* was published in English, it was used at the beginning of the research and, later, checked for content and accuracy against the more recent, Kirundi version, *The Book of Discipline 2011*.

and provide weekly offerings. At each Sunday worship service, baskets are set out and a time is reserved for the calling for offerings. Currently, many local churches and parishes set out a special basket to raise funds for assistance to the most needy in the local church and community.

Tithes and Offerings

The support of the Church, the church income, comes from the tithes, offerings and special offerings or gifts of its members. Considering the tithes, church members are taught at the grass root level to support the church by paying tithes and offerings regularly. Tithes are paid monthly while offerings are paid weekly during church service. The local tithes and offerings are the primary source of income that permits the Free Methodist Church of Burundi to be self-supporting and cover its operating expenses for services, salaries, administration expenses, building expenses and other expenses.

More than 90% of the population of Burundi lives in the country or rural areas as subsistence farmers. In the country or rural areas where the population is mostly made up of subsistence farmers, tithing occurs basically in one of the following two ways. As the first method, tithing might be done seasonally through presenting of some cultivated products such as cassava, beans, rice, potatoes, bananas, or other agricultural products or, perhaps, giving a chicken or even a goat. There are two seasons for harvesting in Burundi; the end of the rainy season, January and February, and the beginning of the dry season, June and July. It is, however, important to notice that offering food stuffs to the church in the minds of many rural church members mainly represents the idea of providing food provisions to the house of the Lord, (Malachi 3:10) or obeying the command of "giving the firstfruits of their harvest" to the Lord (Leviticus 23:10; Numbers 18:12). Then, the local church leadership might keep some of the food for their own use or they might sell some of it to acquire some pay or they might sell the remaining portion for the support of the local church, salaries and local church expenses. It should be recognized that this first way of tithing is done with much variation throughout the country and it seems to have been more common in the past. As for the second way, church members might sell part of their harvest and tithe on a monthly basis just as it is done in the urban areas. The routine of tithing on a monthly basis might have been established through the practice of keeping a membership card which has a 12-month grid for keeping the tithing record.

In the urban areas, tithing takes place on a monthly basis and involves money. During the church services, there is a time reserved for offerings. Once a month, two baskets are set out at the front of the church and members present their tithes in one basket and their offerings in another. In some particular local churches a third basket is also set out for assistance to the most needy.

In both the country and urban areas, each full member has a membership card. The local church leadership records all the tithing on the membership cards.

Another method of tithing is by seeing the local church leader in person and having the leader record the gifts on the membership card. Tithes can also be presented to the church accountant who has the right to issue a receipt and record the gift on the membership card.

Beyond the regular tithes and offerings, the members are also encouraged to give freewill and thanksgiving offerings. In addition, there are special occasion, mandatory offerings for Easter, Pentecost, Christmas and church building projects which are recorded on the membership card. All of the proceeds from offerings, scheduled tithing and special occasion offerings remain at the local level to support the local church and the parish.

Local churches are organized into parishes, usually two to four or five local churches,[7] and a portion of the local offerings, regular tithing and special occasion offerings are used to support the parish expenses. For the budgets at the district, the annual conferences and the general conference levels, full members are expected to pay an additional annual amount, depending on the established budgets and the financial circumstances. The amount has been traditionally labeled in the local language as "Komferensi" which stands for "Conference" or clearly put "Contribution for the Conference." Even the rural illiterate church members feel the responsibility to regularly pay the "Komferensi" and they understand that the money is used for the running of the annual conference activities. For the year 2014, the amount was between 1,000 FBU to 3,000 FBU. The money is given at the local level, transferred to the district level, then, a portion is transferred to the annual conference level and another transfer is made to the general conference level.

As indicated above, there are budgets at the district, the annual conference and general conference levels. These levels are supported by money that is transferred from the lower level to the next level; the local to the parish, the parish to the district, the district to the annual conference and the conference to the general conference. The districts, annual conferences and general conference each have budgets that cover their expenses which are primarily made up of salaries and administration.

The Free Methodist Church of Burundi is self-supporting

---

7. *The Book of Discipline* does not set the number of local churches in a parish but the Annual Conference, during its annual conference, admits a new parish upon request from a particular District and after evaluation of needs and necessity.

as described above. The Church income is generated by regular tithing, offerings and special occasion offerings at the local church level. The tithing, offerings and special offerings cover the expenses of the self-supporting church. The expenses are largely construction (building and repairs), service and training expenses and relatively little for salaries (pastors, deacons, catechists and lay leaders). All pastors and catechists receive some salary, even if it is very small. Lay leaders who are not catechists receive no salary. The salaries for the church leadership are set and paid, according to the budget fixed by the Board of Administration at any level of the Church. Of course, there are expenses at the local, parish, district, conference and general conference levels.

Foreign Funds

The Free Methodist Church of Burundi is a full, independent and self-supporting General Conference. There are no operational funds that are regularly provided to Burundi from the United States of America or Canada or elsewhere. The Free Methodist Church of Burundi does receive some foreign funding from overseas for special appeals for building repairs, building new churches and supporting special services and special events.

The Book of Discipline stipulates that all appeals being made outside an annual conference by local churches must first be cleared by the Board of Administration of the conference into which area the appeal is to be sent. Accordingly, the General Conference does receive some financial support from foreign sources for approved appeals. The "income" from foreign funds; foreign donations for special purposes, is a relatively small amount compared to the income from the local churches.[8]

8. The General Conference budget for September 1, 2013 to August 31, 2014

Although there are no longer any permanent missionaries to Burundi, the Church has some visitors; either missionaries or friends of the Church, who come to serve voluntarily in different areas and fields of the Church. Some are short time, self-supporting missionaries serving in medical areas. Others come to teach at Mweya Theological Institute and Hope Africa University. All of these visitors cover their expenses using their own money or money that they raised independently to support their temporary work.

The Free Methodist Church of Burundi receives some financial assistance from foreign sources and some self-supporting foreign visitors. However, the Free Methodist Church of Burundi is a fully self-supporting church.

II A SELF-PROPAGATING INDIGENOUS ORGANIZATION

Haley wanted to build an indigenous church; a self-propagating indigenous church. The Free Methodist Church of Burundi is self-propagating.

The propagation of the Free Methodist Church of Burundi begins with church members and others at the local church and parish levels.

Members and Membership

There is no better measure of the effectiveness of self-propagation for a church than the growing number of its members. Yearly statistics show a steady and continuous growth in the membership of the indigenous Free Methodist Church of Burundi. As stated above, the indigenous Free Methodist Church of Burundi currently has a membership of

---

indicates that the income from international sources was 16.6% of the total income budget.

155,207; a membership that far exceeds the Free Methodist membership for North America.⁹

Included among their explicit responsibilities, pastors are required to provide an exact count of all members to the Annual Conference for publication in the statistical report and recording the number of local elders, local deacons, local ministerial candidates and lay ministers. Superintendents are expected to ensure that the permanent record book of each society (parish) is kept up-to-date.

Local Churches and Parishes

The indigenous Free Methodist Church of Burundi has 948 local churches (242 parishes). The growing number of local churches and the growing local church membership represent the outcome of self-propagation and provide personnel to extend its self-propagation. As members of an evangelical church, spiritually mature faithful members are expected to participate in evangelizing and winning new souls for Christ and, thereby, contribute to the growth of the church. In order to ensure leadership for evangelism and church growth, the local churches and parishes have pastors, local preachers and lay ministers.

The local churches and parishes are expected to have a Board of Evangelism and Church Growth that develops goals and objectives for evangelism and church growth, plans for needs in personnel, develops strategies to sponsor church

---

9. For 2014, the United States and Canada had a total of 77,420 Free Methodist Church members. According to a telephone enquiry to the Free Methodist Church USA, there were 70,655 Free Methodist Church USA members in 2014 (to be published in the Year Book 2014). According to the Free Methodist Church in Canada website, there were 6,765 members in 2014. See Free Methodist Church in Canada. "FMCIC Statistics." http://fmcic.ca/statistics/. September 24, 2015. Burundi has more members than North America, even if all of northern Latin America is included.

planting in adjacent communities and cooperates with the conference Board of Evangelism and Church Growth activities.

The local churches and parishes are expected to have a Board of Missions that coordinates all church missions programs and pursues a year-round program of mission activities in cooperation with the Board of Administration of the General Conference.

Districts and Conferences

The Free Methodist Church of Burundi currently has 41 districts and 2 conferences. To provide leadership and coordination to evangelism and church growth within the districts, the District Councils elect directors of Children's Ministries, Youth Ministries and Adult Ministries. In addition, the District Councils hold camp meetings that contribute to evangelism and church growth.

The Annual Conferences elect an Evangelism Committee to assist local churches. The Evangelism Committee is required to develop a strategy for church planting, identify communities for church planting, challenge churches operating in the area to sponsor a church planting project, evaluate progress in church growth and provide training and church growth resources.

With the approval of the Conference Board of Evangelism, the Conference Ministerial Appointments Committee appoints Conference Evangelists, entitled to the same rights and privileges of those appointed to pastoral charges, but are only different with regard to their respective assignments. In addition, Lay Ministers with special ministries such as music or personal evangelism may be appointed as Conference Lay Evangelists. The Ministerial Appointments Committee may appoint Church Planters by requesting a local church to sponsor a church planting project or by creating a new church planting project.

Each Annual Conference elects a Missions Committee to conduct conference-wide missions activities and encourage local churches in their missions programming. The Conference Missions Committee promotes broad participation in mission projects, challenges individuals to missionary service and attempts to increase financial support of worldwide missionary outreach.

General Conference

The Board of Administration shall constitute the Board of Evangelism with authority over the Commission on Evangelism. The Commission on Evangelism is responsible for propagation of the church, the evangelization of Burundi and its surrounding countries and areas assigned to it by the General Conference or Board of Administration.

The Board of Administration constitutes the General Missionary Board with authority over the Commission on Missions. The Commission on Missions is responsible for all missionary work outside Burundi and works in partnership with the national church in evangelization and church planting.

Leadership Personnel

The local churches have one or more pastors and pastors play an important role in self-propagation; pastors are involved in propagation and leading propagation and church planting. The indigenous Free Methodist Church currently has 485 pastors, most of whom are local church pastors. The local pastors lead self-propagation and church planting with the support and involvement of members, deacons, catechists, evangelists, catechists and cell group members.

In addition to the local church members and local church leaders, the Free Methodist Church of Burundi has personnel at other levels. At the district and annual conference levels, there are superintendents, evangelists and program leaders. All of these Church leaders are expected to participate in church propagation through evangelism, church planting and missions work.

Training

Training takes place at the local church level. New members receive training and there is catechism training for local church leaders. The local churches are involved in supporting ministerial candidates; currently, there are 85 ministerial candidates.

The Mweya Theological Institute or Institut de Théologie Évangélique de Mweya (I.T.E.M.), founded in 1950, has greatly contributed to the Burundi church self-propagation in training a steady stream of pastors and leaders year after year. Pastors and ministerial candidates also do receive training through Theological Education by Extension (T.E.E.). In addition, the Department of Theology at Hope Africa University, a Free Methodist liberal arts university, provides pastoral and theological degrees.

III A SELF-GOVERNING INDIGENOUS ORGANIZATION

Haley wanted to build an indigenous church; a self-governing indigenous church. The Free Methodist Church of Burundi is self-governing.

The Book of Discipline 2011 states that the Free Methodist Church of Burundi is self-governing.[10] There is

---

10. See Free Methodist Church of Burundi, *The Book of Discipline 2011*, Bujumbura: Free Methodist Church of Burundi, 2011, p. 8.

self-governance at the local church or parish level, the District level, the Annual Conference level and the General Conference level. The governance is participatory, democratic and representative. Not surprisingly, the self-governance of the indigenous Free Methodist Church of Burundi begins at the local church level.

Local Church Level Governance, Official Board

The first and most participatory level of self-governance of the Free Methodist Church of Burundi is with the local members at the local church or parish level. Each local church or society (a local parish with more than one church) has an Official Board. Whenever practical, the Official Board meets once a month if it is possible. The Pastor is the chairperson of the Official Board and is an ex officio member of all boards and committees. The latest edition of Robert's Rules of Order is the standard for the parliamentary procedure of the Official Board.

The Official Board is comprised of only full members; pastors, local preachers, lay ministers and representation from the following areas: Christian growth (class) leaders, the committee on social issues, the committee in charge of the church property, missions, evangelism, finance, church delegates (when needed), teens and other members at large as the society may determine.

The Official Board elects a Secretary to keep minutes and record all marriages and baptisms and a Treasurer to keep records of all of the money raised and all of the expenditures. Depending on the size of the congregation and amount of money, it is recommended that the Official Board elect and define the responsibilities of a Finance Secretary. It is recommended that the Official Board elect members of the church to work with the Pastor and Treasurer as a Finance Committee.

The Official Board provides a Board of Christian Education, a Board of Missions and a Membership Care Committee. The Official Board elects members of the Board of Evangelism and Church Growth, the Pastor's Cabinet and the Board of Stewards. The Official Board serves as the agency for licensing local ministerial candidates according to established guidelines.

District Council Level Governance

To coordinate and administer the Free Methodist Church of Burundi at the district level, the local churches, parishes and Official Boards are organized into District Councils. The District Council holds as many sessions each year as it deems necessary. The District Superintendent is the President of the District Council and presides over the District Council. The latest edition of Robert's Rules of Order is the standard for the parliamentary procedure of the District Council.

The District Council is composed of all pastors of the District, the ministerial candidates, the lay delegates to the previous Annual Conference session and all Departments and Committee leaders at the District level. The Superintendent presides over the District Council.

The District Council elects a Secretary to keep proceedings records and Annual District Council records. The District Council elects a Treasurer. The District Council elects District Directors of Christian education; Children's Ministries, Youth Ministries and Adult Ministries. In cooperation with the Superintendent, the District Council shall appoint and hold camp meetings.

Annual Conference Level Governance

To coordinate and administer the Free Methodist Church of Burundi at the conference level, the districts are organized into Annual Conferences.

There are two Annual Conferences: the Western Conference and the Eastern Conference. The Annual Conference is comprised of all pastors of the conference (including retired pastors) together with an equal number of lay delegates from each district, the Bishop and the substitute legal representative. The Annual Conference meets once a year. The Bishop presides over the Annual Conference. The latest edition of Robert's Rules of Order is the standard for the parliamentary procedure of the Official Board.

The Annual Conference elects a Secretary, a Treasurer and Auditors who give report to the Annual Conference. The Annual Conference elects a Christian Education Committee, an Evangelism Committee, a Missions Committee, a Committee on Social Issues and Ministries and a Board of Stewardship and Finance.

General Conference Level Governance

To coordinate and administer the Free Methodist Church of Burundi, there is a General Conference every five years. The General Conference includes the Bishop, the Annual Conference Superintendents, twelve ministerial delegates and thirteen lay delegates elected by each Annual Conference. The Provisional Kenyan Conference will be represented by six delegates, and the team should include the Bishop and two Annual Conference Superintendents. The General Conference shall elect by ballot one or more traveling elders to serve as pastoral overseers of various areas of the denomination. It shall also elect the Substitute Legal Representative, the Executive Secretary and the Director of Finance and treasurer at the General Conference level. All other senior workers of the General Conference shall be elected by the Board of Administration.

The General Conference is the only legislative body in the church; it has the power to conduct referenda and make rules and regulations. The latest edition of Robert's Rules of Order is the standard for the parliamentary procedure of the General Conference.

The General Conference elects a Board of Administration with general organizational, promotional and supervisory powers over all activities of the church between General Conference sessions. The Board of Administration meets once a year. The Bishop is the President of the Board of Administration.

The Board of Administration elects a Board of Directors of the Free Methodist Foundation to act as trustee for all trusts within the Free Methodist Church of Burundi. The Board of Administration forms an Executive Committee and elects a Budget and Finance Committee.

The Board of Administration establishes an Administrative Commission to oversee appeals, sets bishop and executive salaries, administers the pension plan and oversees social ministry institutions and the Burundi Free Methodist Literature Center. The Board of Administration establishes commissions on Christian Education, Evangelism and Missions.

SUMMARY AND CONCLUSION

Overall, the indigenous Free Methodist Church of Burundi functions very well. In spite of the economic and political challenges in Burundi, the Free Methodist Church of Burundi has definitely and effectively been self-supporting, self-propagating and self-governing. The local churches provide the income to support the local, district, conference and general conference level expenses. The members, pastors and other church leaders ensure the membership continuously and impressively grows. The democratic participation at the local level and the democratic representation at the district, conference and general conference levels ensure the church is completely and successfully self-governing.

In starting my activities as the Bishop of the Free Methodist Church of Burundi in July 2014, the Executive Secretary, Rev. Evariste Bimenyimana, and I met with all superintendents. From September to mid-December, we visited districts. During those visits, we were able to meet all district superintendents, pastors and lay leaders. The purpose was to learn from them, especially to identify needs so that as we start the work we know the needs to meet.

In January 2015, we started to design a 10-year strategic plan on the basis of our consultations and the needs in the Church. It was on June 26, 2015 that the Board of Administration of Burundi Free Methodist General Conference approved the strategic plan which will be the roadmap of our activities during the ten years to come.

The strategic plan is designed to enhance and strengthen the indigenous Free Methodist Church of Burundi; it will reinforce the self-support, self-propagation and self-governance.[11] The strategic plan begins with a SWOT analysis (Strengths, Weaknesses, Opportunities and Threats), followed by statements on the Vision, Mission, Character (values), Skills and Knowledge of the Church. The plan describes the context for the work and identifies four major purposes, programs and related departments to address the context, the

---

11. See the strategic plan; Free Methodist Church of Burundi. *Burundi FMC Ten Years 2016-2025 Strategic Plan Summary*. Bujumbura: Free Methodist Church of Burundi, 2015.

needs and strengthen the indigenous Free Methodist Church of Burundi.

- Evangelism, Discipleship and Church Growth
- Christian Education and Leadership
- Development Local Church Mobilization and Community Transformation
- Free Methodist Church General Development

For each of the four major program areas, the strategic plan provides Goals, Ministries, Activities and Timelines. To lead the work within each program area, the plan identifies a Department and an indigenous Director's position with a detailed Job Description.

To work with the Departments and Directors, the strategic plan seeks foreign volunteer Advisors and a foreign volunteer Manager as shown below. For each volunteer Advisor and the volunteer Manager, the plan outlines a detailed Job Description.

- Adviser/Christian-Theological Education and Curriculum Development
- Adviser/Finances, Grant Writing and Fund Mobilization
- Adviser/Social Work and Sustainable Community Development
- Adviser/Community and Public Health
- Adviser/Leadership, Management and Capacity Building
- Manager/Public Relations and Communication

To support the success of the implementation of the 10-year strategic plan, we request your continuing moral, volunteer and financial support. As you continue to support the indigenous Burundi Free Methodist Church, there are two major prayer needs; the need for volunteer people to come to Burundi and work alongside us and the need for donations to support the implementation of the strategic plan.

As the first Free Methodist Church missionary to Burundi, Haley's vision of an indigenous church and the foundation for an indigenous church have been realized and maintained. There is no doubt Haley would consider the Free Methodist Church of Burundi to be an indigenous church. The legacy of a self-supporting, self-propagating and self-governing organization will continue long into the future. As done in the past, the indigenous Free Methodist Church of Burundi will endure the current political unrest and current tests to democracy, and the Church will continue to function as an exemplary self-supporting, self-propagating, self-governing and democratically self-determining indigenous organization; the indigenous Free Methodist Church of Burundi. With your continuing support, your involvement and the diligent implementation of the 10-year strategic plan, the indigenous Free Methodist Church of Burundi will become a more effective organization; an enhanced and stronger indigenous Free Methodist Church of Burundi.

4

The Mission Temporary, The Church Permanent

Dan Sheffield

Dan Sheffield [1]

In reflecting on John Wesley Haley's missiology, in principle and practice, as articulated in this unfinished manuscript,[2] I would like to identify the particular international mission context at the time of his writing. What was going on in the world as he was writing? To set Haley's missionary career in that same context. Where does Haley fit in the flow of early 20th century mission streams? To examine the specific influences that he mentions in the manuscript. Who were these figures whose writing and ideas played such a significant role in his mission development? And then finally to summarize his missiological framework as represented in the manuscript. What is Haley saying and does it have any meaning for our present context?

---

1. Rev. Dan Sheffield is Director of Global and Intercultural Ministries for The Free Methodist Church in Canada. He has served as a missionary church planter and theological educator in Egypt and South Africa. Dan is an adjunct lecturer at Tyndale Seminary (Toronto, ON, Canada) and Northern Seminary (Lombard, IL, USA
2. On p. 58 of the manuscript, Haley refers to this document as a "brochure;" while his distribution method is unknown, his intended audience was "especially board members and executives directing missionary efforts...," presumably of mission agencies or denominational structures.

Haley's Manuscript in Context

J W Haley was preparing the manuscript that we are examining in this treatment [*The Manuscript: Building the Indigenous Church*] at the time of his death in 1951. The topic, in both principle and practice, had been a part of his life for many decades already. This same topic, however, was also on the minds of other mission leaders at that particular moment in world mission history.

Haley and his family had weathered the Second World War (1939-45)[3] in Burundi (a Belgian protectorate), after returning in 1940 from a furlough assignment in Canada, and then had finally retired back to North America in 1946 in his 68th year. This was, of course, a great period of strife on the international stage. The Haley's own son, Blake, serving with the South African Forces had been captured by the Germans in North Africa before escaping to British-controlled Egypt.

In the manuscript Haley quotes from the International Missionary Council (IMC) meetings in 1947 held at Whitby, Ontario, Canada. The IMC was a broadly-based working group that developed following the World Missionary Conference of 1910 in Edinburgh, Scotland.[4] It is evident from the manuscript that Haley was up-to-date and conversant with the issues before the IMC at the Whitby event. One of the papers presented by Anglican Bishop Stephen Neill, "The Church in a Revolutionary World," specifically addressed the concern to develop self-propagating and self-governing churches.[5] Haley references this address in the manuscript.

---

3. At one point Italian forces were moving toward Burundi, then turned back.
4. The IMC was formed in 1921 as a follow-up from Edinburgh 1910; it eventually (1961) became the mission commission of the World Council of Churches (WCC) which was founded in 1948.
5. Stephen C Neill, "The Church in a Revolutionary World," *International Review of Mission*, V36 (4) October 1947, 434-451.

Likewise, Haley seems to have processed and incorporated the work that proceeded from the IMC Conference in Tambaram/Madras, India in 1938. While much is made of the debate over religious plurality and inter-faith dialogue at Tambaram,[6] Haley and others were more interested in the conversation regarding self-propagation and self-government.[7] He quotes from J Merle Davis' 600 page compilation, *The Economic Basis of the Church*, one of the reports delivered to the conference, and *The Church in the New Jamaica*, a follow-up research project published in 1942.[8]

When Haley retired from Burundi in 1946, the principles and practices required for developing indigenous churches were obviously still on his mind, as his work on this manuscript attests.

It would seem however, that the catalyst required for Haley to write down and organize his principles and practice was occasioned by a particular invitation. Haley, a Canadian, although living at the moment in Cleveland, home of his daughter Florence and her family, was invited to speak at an American mission symposium. At the Chicago conference of the newly-organized Evangelical Foreign Mission Association (EFMA), in April 19-22, 1949, three veteran missionaries presented their thoughts on the notion of

6. Thomas JJ Altizer, "Mission and Dialogue: 50 years after Tambaram," *Christian Century*, April 6, 1988, 340.
7. "At the Tambaram Conference, 'the most representative Christian assembly convened to that time,' more than half the participants came from what was later called the third world. New voices were heard, claiming self-government and self-propagation – and looking toward eventual self-support," John Garrett, *Footsteps in the Sea: Christianity in Oceania to World War II*, Institute of Pacific Studies, World Council of Churches, 1992, 334.
8. Given his affinity for Davis' work, he may also have read *New Buildings on Old Foundations: a handbook on stabilizing the younger churches in their environment*, New York: IMC, 1945.

developing indigenous church practices.[9] J W Haley, at age 71, spoke on "How to Establish the Indigenous Church;" Dr T S Soltau, a Presbyterian missionary for many years in Korea, spoke on "The Missionary and the Indigenous Church;"[10] and Rev M L Hodges, an Assemblies of God missionary in Central America, spoke on "How May the Mission Assist the Indigenous Church."[11]

Following their presentations there was such a positive response that the organizing committee was asked to have a greater focus on this topic at their convention the following year.[12]

9. The Evangelical Foreign Mission Association (EFMA) was organized in 1946 as an initiative of the US-based National Association of Evangelicals (NAE). The NAE was formed in 1942/43, largely as a response to the polarized 'fundamentalist' groups in the American Council of Christian Churches (ACCC) and the mainline 'modernist' groups in what would become the National Council of Churches (NCC). [see also, Harold Lindsell, "An Appraisal of Agencies not cooperating with the International Missionary Council grouping," *International Review of Mission*, 47, No 186, Apr 1958, 202-209.] The Free Methodist Church joined the NAE in this early period, and therefore were active participants in the EFMA from its beginnings.
10. Korea was the location of the most successful implementation of the Nevius Plan for developing indigenous churches, from 1893 onwards.
11. *EFMA Minutes*, April 20, 1949, 3
12. Despite this intention of follow-up on indigenous church principles it would seem that the EFMA did not again address this topic in a substantial manner until the Green Lake, Wisconsin conference in 1971, where some (Orlando Costas, *The Church and Its Mission: a shattering critique from the Third World*, Wheaton: Tyndale House, 1974) would suggest it was not addressed adequately. At a joint EFMA/IFMA meeting in Wheaton in 1966, "the conference confessed in its statement that church growth is hindered by "too much missionary control, too much dependence on paid workers." And it admitted that it has perpetuated paternalism and provoked "unnecessary tensions between national churches and missionary societies." The addition of "paternalism" to the evangelical vocabulary is another hopeful sign. But it will take more than diagnosis to rid the body of the disease. These mission societies are plagued by paternalism because, in many cases, they have a low concept of

Another result of this Chicago event was the publication of a pamphlet by the EFMA highlighting the indigenous church principles.[13] (Editor John McCready has included Haley's portion of that pamphlet as the summarizing chapter for this posthumously published version of Haley's writing project.)

A note in the EFMA follow-up pamphlet indicates that "the increase in nationalism throughout the world demands an understanding of this method."[14] This is certainly a reference to the collapse of several colonial systems at that moment, particularly in India, Pakistan (1947), Palestine/Israel, Burma, Ceylon (1948), Indonesia, Laos and China (1949), where mission support systems often paralleled empire infrastructure centered upon a Western 'head office.' Many mission agencies and denominations were wondering if their mission churches would survive the de-colonization era. In the manuscript Haley himself references, "the rising tide of nationalism in the East" (94) and mentions the slogan, "the white man out of Asia."[15]

All of these elements, coming together at this moment, would have been feeding into Haley's frame of reference as he worked on the manuscript. It is unfortunate that he was not able to finish the work, as it was certainly a timely exercise. Several years later, both of the other speakers at

---

the church," Maynard Shelley, "Evangelical Congress on Worldwide Mission," *Christian Century*, 83, No 21, May 25, 1966, 695-697.

13. *The Indigenous Church: The Biblical Method of Missions* published by UEA, 1949. Haley's portion was first published in *United Evangelical Action*, Vol 8 (13) Aug 15, 1949, 5-6.
14. Ibid.
15. A statement made by Toshio Shiratori, an official advisor to Japan's Foreign Office in 1940, and former ambassador to Italy (1938-40): "Japan's true aim was to drive the white man out of Asia," quoted in Gerald Horne, *Race War: White Supremacy and the Japanese Attack on the British Empire*, New York University Press, 2004, 82.

the 1949 EFMA conference published books on the subject.[16] Pentecostal missionary Melvin Hodges, would publish *The Indigenous Church* (1953), which would become the standard evangelical mission text on this subject for years to come.

Knowing as we do that Haley would die with this "brochure" unpublished, it is fitting to note his purposes in writing. These would be his final thoughts on the challenge of "building an indigenous church." His target audience was twofold – "board members and executives directing missionary efforts," and "those who are enlisted in the cause, or soon to join the present crusade to make Christ known" (fellow missionaries).[17]

His purpose, "with the conviction that what I have gleaned during the fifty years since I volunteered for pioneer missionary effort, should be made available..." was "to incite a study of New Testament order, which is illustrated by the presence of expanding, spontaneous churches in many parts of the world." Mission executives, in particular, "should be informed on methods that fail and methods that succeed."[18]

Tellingly, his effort in this manuscript (left unpublished) and his consistent advocating of indigenous methodology, over many years previously, went largely unheeded by the Free Methodist Mission.[19]

---

16. Melvin L Hodges, *The Indigenous Church: a complete handbook on how to grow young churches*, Springfield, MO: Gospel Publishing House, 1976 (revised edition). T Stanley Soltau, *Missions at the Crossroads*, Wheaton: Van Kempen Press, 1954.
17. *Manuscript*, 48.
18. Ibid.
19. Dr Philip Capp, who entered Free Methodist missionary service in Southern Africa in 1957 until his retirement in 1995, had no recollection of teaching on, or discussion of, the work of J W Haley in regards to indigenous mission practices; personal conversation, May 23, 2012. Haley's work presently seems to be regarded fondly. Bishop Gerald Bates, former missionary to Burundi wrote, "Haley was the principal founder of arguably the greatest mission

Haley, the Missionary, in context

Haley's manuscript represents his mature reflections on mission practice at what would be the very end of his life. We note his references to earlier points in his missionary career where he understood little of the task set before him, and also decisive moments of correction to both his understanding and his practice. To continue to place Haley's manuscript in context, outlining his thoughts on the development of indigenous churches, it would be appropriate to add some comments on his intellectual development over time.

Not wanting to go over territory covered in previous biographical work on Haley,[20] I will restrict my comments to historical and social contexts directly referenced in the manuscript.

Early Ministry Development (1900-1917)

Haley states, unequivocally in Chapter V of the manuscript, that as a young 23-year-old missionary he had almost no clue what he was doing when he was sent out as a missionary, other than to "preach the Gospel to the heathen." And likewise the mission structure of the Free Methodist Church did not have "any clearer conception of the purpose of my going."

Haley did, however, have the experience of two years of pioneer church planting work in Saskatchewan prior to his departure for Africa.[21] In his work as "an assistant" to

---

initiative in Free Methodist history in terms of fruitfulness. A large and growing harvest continues to this day." "John Wesley Haley: Prophet and Apostle," *Free Methodist Historical Society Newsletter*, Summer 2001, Vol. 2, No. 1, 1.

20. Gerald Bates, *Soul Afire: The Life of J W Haley*, Winona Lake, IN: Light and Life Press, 1981.

21. Haley worked alongside Rev W H Wilson in southern Saskatchewan (1900-01), an area just being opened up to new settlement, with many people

an ordained minister he learned the significance of an apprenticeship in ministry. It was only after a year of experience in Saskatchewan, at age 22, that he was recognized with a local minister's license,[22] the first level of accreditation toward ordained ministry in the Free Methodist Church. A year later he was on his way to Africa. Haley thus had some understanding of the nature of the church, experience in the development of embryonic Christian communities, and the reality of new, self-supporting, congregations.

In reflecting on his first five years in Mozambique, in a very early publication, Haley stated that "the work is done by the natives themselves, the missionaries simply superintending them..."[23] In fact, "in many ways an evangelist is better qualified to open up new work than a missionary. If we go to a community where the Gospel has never been preached, the people flock to look at the white man. Our hearts may be breaking as we tell them the story of Jesus and his love, but notwithstanding our best efforts to lift up Christ, they see us and nothing else."[24]

Haley goes on to suggest that "we are aiming at self-support in our churches, and expect some of the older out-stations will soon be self-sustaining."[25] Here we have Haley, in 1907, using the language of 'indigenous church' methodology very early in his missionary service, certainly prior to any interaction with Roland Allen's work that he references in the foreword to the manuscript.

It is possible that Haley had already had contact with the

    moving from southern Ontario. He was responsible for the early development of the Westview congregation.
22. Annual Conference, 1901.
23. J W Haley, "Our work at Inhambane from 1902 to 1907," in Chloe Brodhead (ed.), *Free Methodist Missions in Africa*, Pittsburgh, PA: Aldine Printing Co. 1908, 20
24. Ibid., 20.
25. Ibid., 22.

work of Henry Venn (CMS) and Rufus Anderson (ABCFM), who coined the classic "three-self" definition of the indigenous church.[26] Presbyterian missionary John Nevius of China and Korea had published a model[27] that eventually became known as "The Nevius Plan."[28] Another Presbyterian missionary, Robert Speer, had just recently (1902) published an update on these principles as well.[29]

After almost 8 years of ministry, in 1909 the Haley family returned to Canada for health reasons, as it seemed Haley himself was suffering the ongoing effects of a malaria infection. It would not be until 1917 that they returned to Africa. Free Methodist Bishop Hogue, writing in 1915, summarized this first term of service: Haley "always stood high among the missionaries, and was among the most successful of them."[30]

During this hiatus, however, we must not imagine Haley as reclining in some convalescent facility. He and his young family returned to Canada where he took up farming 634 acres in southern Saskatchewan[31] for a period of four years as his body recovered strength. One of the results of their time

---

26. Wilbert R. Shenk, "Rufus Anderson and Henry Venn: A Special Relationship?" *International Bulletin of Missionary Research* 5, (4) (1981), 168.
27. See John L Nevius, *The Planting and Development of Missionary Churches*, Shanghai: Presbyterian Press, 1886; 3rd edition published in 1899 by Foreign Mission Library, New York.
28. Charles A Clark, *The Nevius Plan for Mission Work*, Christian Literature Society, 1937.
29. Robert E Speer, *Missionary Principles and Practices*, New York: Fleming Revell, 1902.
30. William Hogue, *The History of the Free Methodist Church of North America (Vol.II)*, Chicago: Free Methodist Publishing House, 1915, 277
31. St. Boswells, SK; *The Annual Minutes: Proceedings of the Forty Annual Conferences of the Free Methodist Church of North America*, Chicago: The Free Methodist Publishing House, 1910, 385.

on the prairies was a new church plant in the village of St Boswells.[32] In 1913, when Haley was 35, the family moved to Ontario where he served in pastoral ministry in Niagara Falls for a period of time before settling in Sarnia for several years.

Also of note during this period of absence from the work in Africa is Haley's participation in the work of the World Missionary Conference (WMC) held in Edinburgh, Scotland in 1910. In the preparation stage for the WMC, organizers J H Oldham and John R Mott, initiated an extensive research project to understand the spread of Christianity in the non-Christian world. As missionaries in South Africa, Haley and his Free Methodist colleague, Rev J P Brodhead, contributed information, and are noted as "correspondents" in the record of the WMC.[33] The Free Methodist Church, itself, was represented at the WMC by Bishop William Pearce, Rev B Winget, Mission Secretary, and Mrs M L Coleman, President, Women's Missionary Society.[34]

Given Haley's interest in the documented work of the International Missionary Council in later years, his own participation in the WMC research, and Free Methodist presence at the Edinburgh event, it would seem highly probable that Haley read the written report of the WMC, or at least some of the many summaries, reports and critiques which went to press following the conference.[35] From literally thousands of pages of content, we can imagine that Haley would have noted the address by Indian leader, V S Azariah

---

32. Annual Conference records record a 'charge' at St Boswells, SK in 1914 and following.
33. Report I, "Carrying the Gospel…," *World Missionary Conference, Appendix A*, Edinburgh, 1910, 390.
34. "Delegates to Conference," *World Missionary Conference, Vol 9*, Edinburgh, 1910, 58.
35. Although it is somewhat difficult to imagine this seasoned missionary and world traveller peering through a mission journal by coal-oil in a homesteader's cabin on the wind-swept prairie!

who said to the missionaries present, "Through all the ages to come the Indian Church will rise up in gratitude to attest the heroism and self-denying labours of the missionary body. You have given your goods to feed the poor. You have given your bodies to be burned. We also ask for love. Give us friends!"[36] This call for respect, collegiality and friendship with national believers was to become a hallmark of the ongoing work of the IMC and would certainly have influenced Haley's thoughts as he interacted with the IMC ministry stream in the decades to come.

It is apparent in later years that Haley understood the thrust of this call for greater partnership and collegiality in ministry with the emerging churches. His openness to the breadth of voices in the Christian community would also remain a distinction. As the Free Methodist Church in North America was gradually influenced more and more by the fundamentalist-modernist polarization that would lead to a rejection of the broader, ecumenical voice of the IMC (and its openness to partnership and indigenous principles), Haley left this theological maelstrom behind to return to South Africa where greater issues were at stake.[37]

---

36. Quoted in Dana Robert, "Cross-Cultural Friendship in the Creation of Twentieth Century World Christianity," *International Bulletin of Missionary Research*, Vol 35 (2) 2011, 100.
37. Haley would continue to flow between these divergent streams, referred to as Fundamentalism and Conciliarism. Fundamentalists (1910 and following) would develop a highly individualized focus on personal conversion, and viewed the world around them, including the diverse cultures found in it, through the pessimistic lens of premillenial-dispensationalist eschatology. Early advocates of the 'social gospel' (Rauschenbusch, 1907) combined the evangelical emphasis on conversion with efforts to reform the structures of society. Many in the Conciliar movement would maintain this framework (Visser't Hooft, Newbigin) in contrast to liberal notions of progressive social transformation. Likewise, various conservative evangelicals, particularly within the Pietist and Holiness churches, did not accept the sharp dichotomy between

The Experienced Missionary/Pastor returns to South Africa (1917-1934)

During Haley's absence from South Africa (1909-1916), momentous actions had taken place in the political and social context of the region. Haley had arrived for his first term of service (1902) immediately following the Anglo-Boer War (1899-1902). In 1910 the British and Boer colonies were brought together as the Union of South Africa, a dominion of the British Empire, an arrangement very similar to that of Haley's own Canada. 1912 would see the founding of the South African Native National Congress, a body concerned with the civil rights of black South Africans that would eventually become the African National Congress.[38] The Natives Land Act of 1913 would restrict black Africans from buying land outside of the "native reserves," which amounted to only 7% of the total land mass of the Union.

Haley returned to the coastal region of southern Natal province, to the Free Methodist mission station at Fairview/Umzumbe. He was 39 years old. In Section VIII of Haley's manuscript – "The Teacher Becomes the Taught," he offers an account of his developing understanding of "the native question."[39] Writing in this manuscript just three years after the founding of the Nationalist government's *apartheid* state (1948), Haley provides a scathing analysis of South Africa's social and political inequities, as well as of contrasting approaches to leadership empowerment within denominational structures.

Haley indicates that, on his return to South Africa, he

'word and deed' that became the hallmark of fundamentalism. Wilbert Shenk, *Changing Frontiers of Mission*, Maryknoll: Orbis, 1999, 22-25.

38. The first black African president of South Africa was Nelson Mandela (1994), a member of the African National Congress.
39. Haley uses the phrase "the native question" seemingly as an intentional misquote of the normal topic reference – "the native problem."

felt it his "duty to get to the bottom of it" – "the native question." He says that he "read widely in an effort to discover its meaning."[40] At the beginning he was "inclined to think the Europeans were dealing fairly with their wards," but as time went by his opinion changed, and with deeper knowledge and greater experience with nationals, he "began to feel that the native question could be visualized as, how to get the most possible out of the Native for the smallest possible return."[41]

In 1922, the Haley family moved from rural Natal province to Benoni, on the outskirts of Johannesburg. Here they would engage with Mozambican believers connected with the FMC back in the Inhambane region and use this as a base for outreach to unbelieving Mozambicans working on the mines. Haley had just arrived at the heart of the South African 'native question,' – the gold mines, and the emerging migrant labour system.

In fact the Haley family arrived one week after the start of the General Strike on the mines in January 1922 which would evolve over the next several months into what became known as the Rand Rebellion, or alternatively as the "Red Revolt."[42] About 22,000 white gold miners went on strike

---

40. A sample of Haley's 'wide' reading may have included: A Davis, *The Native Problem in South Africa*, London: Chapman & Hall, 1903; H Pim, *The Native Problem in South Africa*, Johannesburg, 1905; H J Crocker, *The South African Race Problem: The Solution of Segregation*, Johannesburg, 1908; F W Bell, *The South African Native Problem: A Suggested Solution*, Johannesburg, 1909; H E Rawson, "The Native Problems," *African Affairs*, 1912 XI: 151-172. Haley indicates that early on he had no knowledge of "an African press then," and therefore could not comment on their understanding of the issues. He appears to have missed the seminal work of black African writer, Sol T Plaatje, *Native Life in South Africa: Before and Since the European War and the Boer Rebellion*, London: P S King & Son, 1916.
41. *Manuscript*, 98.
42. See Haley's comments in "Gold, Guns and Government," *Life in Mozambique and South Africa*, Chicago: Free Methodist Publishing House, 1926, 105-113.

protesting "intensified exploitation and a decision by gold-mining industry leaders to replace many white workers with black workers." Striking workers would take over the city of Benoni where the Haleys were residing, resulting in house-to-house searches by government forces and the dropping of bombs from small planes on labour strongholds. The Union government would conclude that "the revolt had been a socialist revolution organized by Bolshevists, international socialists, and Communists."[43]

In the midst of his ongoing ministry, now in peri-urban Johannesburg, Haley was concerned with the notion of opening new work in, as yet, untouched regions. As early as 1923 his *Journal* reflects an interest in Belgian-controlled Central Africa. Through connections with the International Missionary Council in 1924 Haley contacted Dr Henri Anet, the Protestant liaison for mission work in Belgian territories, inquiring about opening a Free Methodist work in Central Africa. In 1925, Haley and his wife were able to meet with Mrs. Priscilla Studd, the wife of C T Studd, pioneer missionary to Belgian-controlled Congo, as she travelled on a speaking tour of South Africa.[44] Haley was inspired by Studd's story of opening new work in Congo at age 52, where they had seen 10,000 baptisms over a period of ten years.[45]

Upon their return to North America on furlough, in 1926, Haley would publish a unique reflection entitled, *Life in Mozambique and South Africa*. While ostensibly an extended

---

43. "The Rand Revolt striker's stronghold at Fordsburg Square falls to government," *South African History Online: toward a People's History*, http://www.sahistory.org.za/dated-event/rand-revolt-strikers039-stronghold-fordsburg-square-falls-government (accessed Nov 25, 2011)
44. C T Studd, formerly a missionary to China, formed the Heart of Africa Mission in 1910; it would shortly be renamed Worldwide Evangelization Crusade (WEC), an independent mission agency today numbering 2000 missionaries, focused on the most unreached regions of the world.
45. Bates, *Soul Afire*, 20

missionary 'newsletter' for the Free Methodist constituency back in North America, Haley also provided anthropological insights on marriage customs, ancestral responsibilities, socials systems, mine compound life, the place of traditional brewing methods and 'Bantu' religious practices. Haley comments on the government's *Report of Native Churches Commission*, an examination of the reasons for the emergence of independent, separatist church movements.[46] "The report traces several of the principal sects to their origin and states that in many cases the unsympathetic attitude of the white missionary is responsible for the breaking away of the native minister and his adherents."[47]

In the preface to *Life in Mozambique and South Africa* Haley references a publication that he viewed as valuable in his writing, "Christianity and the Race Problem."[48] Although he does not cite the author, one is led to believe he is referring to J H Oldham's highly influential book of the same name, just recently published.[49] Oldham, a leader in the International Missionary Council, had produced "a cogently argued rebuttal of 'scientific' racism."[50] An idea popular at the time, "scientific" racism used scientific techniques and hypotheses to sanction the belief in racial superiority, inferiority, and racism. Oldham's book, rather than talking of "'menace" or of "fan[ning] the flames of race hatred and jealousy", advocated that Europeans "cultivate the friendly spirit, help the backward peoples and build up the City of God on this fair

---

46. Haley, *Life*, 130-131; A W Roberts, *Report of Native Churches Commission*, Cape Town, SA: Union of South Africa, 1925.
47. *Life*, 131.
48. Ibid., 9.
49. J H Oldham, *Christianity and the Race Problem*, New York: Doran, 1924.
50. Christine Weir, "White Man's Burden, White Man's Privilege: Christian humanism and racial determinism," in *Foreign Bodies: Oceania and the Science of Race 1750-1940*, ed. B Douglas and C Ballard, Canberra: Australian National University E-Press, 2008, 297.

earth."[51] Oldham asserted that "The differences between men … are differences within a unity. Underlying all differences of race there exists a common humanity."[52] Oldham "saw difference as a good thing, part of God's great variety. But only the growth of true respect and economic equity would counter the growth of hostility."[53]

This perspective surely influenced Haley's own reflection as he wrote, "the development of a native church that will be self-supporting, self-governing and self-propagating must be the final aim of all missionary work." At this point in his thought process, however, he concludes: "Among the Bantu this must be a process covering many years, but the ideal must never be lost sight of." He goes on to cite examples of "remarkable progress" where national Christians did not receive any kind of financial support from overseas. Haley questions mission policy which suggested that monetary payments to "native evangelists" allow the missionaries to maintain control over the national church. He retorts: "This thought is too unworthy to be seriously entertained… money control is the worst kind of control."[54]

It is possible that the opportunity to reflect on African life and his missionary practice in the writing of *Life…* may have solidified Haley's commitment to the indigenous church approach, and his commitment to move elsewhere so as to be able to put it into practice without hindrance. Haley had already taken steps to find a place for Free Methodist ministry in the Great Lakes region before his furlough in 1926, but upon the family's return to South Africa in 1927, this would be his over-arching passion.

51. Ibid, 297.
52. Oldham, 80.
53. Weir, 298.
54. Op. cit., *Life*, 80.

The Mature Missionary: Northward to the Great Lakes (1932-1946)

Haley's eventual move to Burundi in 1934 was an exercise in perseverance over almost a full decade. It is more than possible that his own interaction with The Missionary God, coupled with a sense of the Holy Spirit's intervention and guidance in his affairs, and the extremely difficult family, financial and physical circumstances in which he placed himself would confirm his belief that national church leaders could also succeed with access to the same mission-empowering God that he served.[55]

While his own mission board continually waffled between supporting and thwarting his efforts to open work in the Great Lake region, Haley had ongoing encouragement from the wider mission community. Records document his interaction with leaders in the International Missionary Council (IMC). He had first contacted Rev. Dr. Henri Anet, IMC's liaison with Belgium's *Bureau des Missions Protestantes du Congo Belge*, in 1924.[56] He met with British and Foreign Bible Society personnel in London, 1926, who suggested Burundi as his target location.

In December 1930 Free Methodist mission leaders once again turned down his request for an exploratory trip to the Great Lakes region. A few weeks later, however, in January 1931, Alexander McLeish of World Dominion Movement (Roland Allen's mission research organization), was advocating on Haley's behalf to Dr Anet for a mission location in Burundi.

When Haley was finally approved for an exploratory trip to Belgian Congo he was received in 1932 by Swedish

---

55. For details on this period see, Bates, *Soul Afire*, 17-35
56. Archives, Bureau des Eglises et Missions Protestantes en Afrique Centrale, Bruxelles uu.diva-portal.org/smash/get/diva2:240717/FULLTEXT07 (Accessed Nov 25, 2011)

Pentecostal missionaries and greatly aided by Danish Baptist missionaries as he surveyed the possibilities in Burundi for two weeks.

Shortly after his return to South Africa from this visit, still reflecting on missionary practice as he anticipated a new work opening in Burundi, Haley sent off a letter to Free Methodist Missionary Secretary B L Olmstead:

> "I think all our missionaries should read "The Korean Church and the Nevius Methods" and the new missionaries should pass an examination on it. Then the reading course should include such books as "Missionary Methods: St Paul's or Ours?" and a number of other such books."[57]

Throughout much of 1934 there was a flurry of letters and telegrams between A L Warnshuis of IMC (New York), A McLeish of World Dominion (London), and Dr H Anet (Brussels), all trying to pave the way for Haley and a new Protestant mission group in Burundi.[58]

On Haley's arrival in Burundi in late 1934 to initiate the Free Methodist mission, he was again assisted by Swedish Pentecostal and Danish Baptist missionaries. Soon after starting the new work, a relationship also developed with the National Holiness Missionary Society, the Anglican Church Missionary Society (CMS) and the Friends Africa Gospel Mission where mission stations were mutually cared for by the different bodies regardless of their theological and

---

57. Letter to Olmstead, August 20, 1932, quoted in Bates, *Soul Afire*, 112, referencing Charles Allen Clark, *The Korean Church and the Nevius Methods* (1930), and Roland Allen, *Missionary Methods: St Paul's or Ours?* (1912).
58. Archives, Bureau des Eglises et Missions Protestantes en Afrique Centrale, Bruxelles uu.diva-portal.org/smash/get/diva2:240717/FULLTEXT07 (Accessed Nov 25, 2011)

organizational distinctives. In July 1935, J W Haley became one of the founders of the Protestant Alliance of Ruanda-Urundi. A missionary in the Friends mission group confirms "this Alliance was to become unique in the world, as an example of Christian fellowship and unity of purpose among Protestant Missions."[59]

This collegiality would eventually allow Haley's ideas on indigenous church development to take their place among other mission groups. Although viewed sceptically and as impractical at the beginning, when the war cut off funds that British and Danish missionaries were using to pay their national pastors, Haley was invited to address various gatherings and explain his approach.[60] More than 30 years after Haley left Burundi, World Gospel Church leaders would indicate that "many of the early guiding principles" of their church "were formulated by Haley" and "still govern the present day" work.[61]

The East Africa Revival, beginning about 1940, first emerged in Uganda and Rwanda among the churches associated with the Anglican Church Missionary Society (CMS). This unique ministry of the Holy Spirit, producing confessions of sin and whole-hearted conversions was characterized by openness, transparency, and great personal warmth and love between believers. When the revival moved into Burundi in 1941, Haley's Anglican colleagues were not as familiar with these 'revivalistic' manifestations. At a large conference of the Protestant Alliance, including both

59. Ralph E Choate, *Dust of His Feet: A Short Story of the Friends Africa Gospel Mission*, Mweya, 1965, 13.
60. Bates, *Soul Afire*, 79-80.
61. Donald Hohensee, *Church Growth in Burundi*, Pasadena, CA: William Carey Library, 1977, 48. Hohensee writes: "Rev J W Haley was a seasoned missionary when he came to Burundi and a very godly man. His counsel and advice served to help many a discouraged missionary as well as to challenge the African Church leaders with their task and responsibility," 48.

missionaries and nationals, held at Muyebe (FMC mission) in 1942, Haley played a leading role in bridging the gap. CMS mission leader, Dr A C Stanley Smith wrote to Haley:

> "We in the CMS owe a still greater debt of gratitude because the meetings at Muyebe paved the way to our mission conference at Matana, and there the Lord did great things for us, which humanly speaking might never have happened but for the wider appreciation of revival which your experience gave us."[62]

Now a senior missionary leader in the region (64 years old in 1942), Haley would repeat this investment in the Protestant Alliance community again several years later. Meg Guillebaude, in *Rwanda: The Land God Forgot?* recalls her CMS missionary parents' reflections on those meetings;

> "In 1945 there was a significant gathering of missionaries of all denominations at Mutaho in Burundi. The speaker was J W Haley of the Free Methodists, a real man of God who emphasized the need for the holiness of God to be reflected by holy living. He was concerned about the lack of unity among the Anglican missionaries and called them together to talk over their difficulties."[63]

---

62. Quoted in Bates, *Soul Afire*, 82.
63. Meg Guillebaud, *Rwanda, the Land God Forgot? Revival, Genocide and Hope*, London: Monarch Books, 2002, 115.

It is in this context, of a growing, Holy Spirit-fed, Free Methodist church in Burundi, with the respect of mission colleagues from a variety of traditions – evangelical and conciliar – that Haley would retire to North America in 1946.[64]

Even in retirement however, he continued to prod his own Free Methodist mission leaders: "if the home church were relieved of the support of [indigenous] pastors in the mission fields it would have money to send out more missionaries and open new fields...and do in a word what is their own particular task."[65]

This brings us to the point in Haley's story, where he begins to organize his thoughts, convictions and practices for the EFMA Chicago conference in 1949 in which he serves as a bridge between Edinburgh 1910, the International Missionary

---

64. In the period 1940-1950, the communicant membership of the Free Methodist Church in Burundi grew by a rate of 200% annually; Hohensee, *Church Growth in Burundi*, 75-82.
65. Byron Lamson, *To Catch the Tide*, Winona Lake: General Missionary Board, 1963, 28.

Congress, the strategic work of Anglican and Presbyterian missionaries (Allen and Nevius), and the conservative Evangelical mission community. And then, seemingly energized by that effort, Haley takes on the larger task of preparing the manuscript we are examining, until his death in 1951.

Influences on Haley's Missiology

In seeking to make sense of Haley's missiology we must return to the manuscript where he specifically mentions a number of authors and their writings that had influenced his mission thinking and practice. A brief examination of each of these influencers will prove helpful in understanding Haley's frame of reference.

Christian Scripture

As one reads Haley's manuscript we are struck by his deep engagement with Scripture and biblical theology. Despite the growing influence of liberal, historical-critical methodology upon IMC leaders, Haley maintained an Evangelical view of a God-breathed/inspired Scripture. On the other hand, he does not start with a pragmatic methodology and then seek to find Scripture to support his proposals. He starts with Scripture. Haley roots the first four chapters of his brochure (The Unfinished Task, The Church: God's Instrument for World Redemption, The Gifts of the Spirit, and The Church Inaugurated) in a missional reading of the New Testament. In fact, Haley suggests that it is when missionary methods are separated from Scripture that efforts are "fruitless."[66]

---

66. *Manuscript*, 62.

Roland Allen (1868-1947)

Haley, in the very first paragraph of his manuscript, references Anglican missionary and missiologist, Roland Allen. In particular, Allen's "startling" book, *Missionary Methods: St Paul's or Ours?*[67] Haley cites Allen's perspective on "successful" missionary methods as a contrast to many missionary efforts which fail. In his foreword, Haley says that his purpose in writing is to examine New Testament 'order' which is typified "by the presence of expanding, spontaneous churches in many parts of the world."[68] Haley viewed Allen as a voice that pointed him in the right direction.

Roland Allen was born into the home of an Anglican priest in England. His father, Charles Allen, died in British Honduras, when Roland was only five years old. Following his own ordination as a priest Allen applied to serve as a missionary but was turned down because of poor health. After applying to another mission agency, for service in China, he convinced his doctor to give him a clean bill of health so that he would not be turned down again.

Allen arrived in China in 1895 where he quickly acquired the Mandarin language, a notable accomplishment. He survived the Boxer Rebellion of 1900 while living in Peking. This incident was profoundly disturbing to Allen, who believed it to be a result of the 'foreignness' of the existing mission system and methodology.[69] Following a furlough in 1901, he returned to China with a new bride in 1902. It was during this second term that Allen began to apply some of his emerging principles regarding self-responsibility and

---

67. Roland Allen, *Missionary Methods: St Paul's or Ours?* Grand Rapids: Eerdmans, 1962.
68. In 1927 Allen published, *The Spontaneous Expansion of the Church—and the causes which hinder it*, London: Lutterworth Press, 2006.
69. Shenk, *Changing Frontiers*, 55.

indigenous leadership. But ill health quickly re-appeared and within one year the Allens were back in England where he served as a parish priest and recovered his health. As Allen stated: 'I was ill, and came home for two years, and began to study the methods of the Apostle St. Paul. From that day forward I began to see light."[70]

In 1912, Allen published his classic work *Missionary Methods: St. Paul's or Ours?* In it Allen advocated that the missionary methods of Paul were not ancient history but rather to be applied to missionary activity in any era. Allen stated—'I myself am more convinced than ever that in the careful examination of his [St. Paul's] work, above all in the understanding and appreciation of his *principles,* we shall find the solution of most of our present difficulties.'[71] Near the end of the book, Allen states — 'at any rate this much is certain, that the Apostle's methods succeeded exactly where ours have failed.'[72]

A few years later, Allen, with several others, founded the World Dominion Movement, a mission think tank devoted to research and the dissemination of Allen's principles and practice. This organization published Allen's subsequent books and essays,[73] as well as mission survey research and a regular magazine, *World Dominion.* In the 1930s JW Haley would have direct contact with the World Dominion Movement seeking advice on his move to Ruanda-

---

70. Hubert J B Allen, *Roland Allen: Pioneer, Priest, and Prophet*, Cincinnati, OH: Forward Movement Publications; Grand Rapids, MI: Eerdmans, 1995, 75.
71. Roland Allen, 1962, p.vii.
72. Ibid, 147.
73. *Essential Missionary Principles* (1913), "Pentecost and the World" (1917), *Educational Principles and Missionary Methods* (1919), "Voluntary Clergy" (1923), *The Spontaneous Expansion of the Church and the Causes Which Hinder It* (1927), "Non-professional Missionaries" (1929),

Urundi,[74] suggesting some familiarity with Allen's work beyond *Missionary Methods*.

In the early 1930s Allen and his wife moved to Nairobi, Kenya to be nearer their adult children; the same time period that Haley was settling in nearby Burundi. Despite dealing with emotional depression in his later years largely due to the lack of acceptance of his views, Allen continued to write and remained associated with the Anglican Church; he learned Swahili and translated several Swahili writings into English. Allen died in 1947 at 79 and is buried in Nairobi.[75]

In Haley's manuscript we notice his insistence on methods that can be traced to Scripture, the missional nature of the Church, and the Holy Spirit as the central resource in the development of an indigenous church. Here he is following directly in Allen's footsteps.[76] In both Haley and Allen, one notices a combination of the disciplined use of appropriate methods alongside a profound openness to the 'unplanned' work of the Holy Spirit. Allen states that "Christ had given the apostles a world-wide commission, embracing all the nations; but intellectually they did not understand what He meant. They found that out as they followed the impulse of the Spirit."[77]

While we do not find any direct quotes from Roland

---

74. In the records of Bureau des Eglises et Missions Protestantes en Afrique Centrale, Bruxelles; in 1931, Alexander McLeish of WDM advocates to Dr Henri Anet on behalf of Rev J W Haley of the Free Methodist Mission who was seeking opportunity to open a mission in Belgian-held Ruanda-Urundi; Série 13 : Miscellaneous 1922-1937, 6. Ruanda Burundi Gouv., 1922–1931, http://uu.diva-portal.org/smash/get/diva2:240717/FULLTEXT07 , accessed Nov 18, 2011.
75. This basic outline of Allen's life is derived from: J D Payne, "The Legacy of Roland Allen," *The Churchman*, Vol 117 (4) 2003, 315-328.
76. Payne, 321.
77. Roland Allen, "Pentecost and the World," pamphlet published by World Dominion Movement, 1917.

Allen's many publications in Haley's manuscript, it is safe to assume that Haley's prominent reference to Allen's work in the Foreword would indicate a significant interplay between the thinker and the practitioner. One common feature is an approach that is more directly focused on historical, biblical and theological factors, rather than a specific examination of cultural or sociological factors,[78] although Haley certainly does touch on these, as well as providing examples of specific practices from his own experience. Another overlap is their approach to "devolution," the practice of a gradual handover of rights, authority and privileges to the national church over an arbitrary time period. Both Allen and Haley insisted on a "from the start" approach.[79]

It is commonly suggested that Allen was a man ahead of his time. Many of his perspectives were set aside by mission leaders and practitioners during his own lifetime, while being recovered and appreciated decades after.[80] There is no record of contact between Haley and Allen despite their proximity in Africa for at least a decade. Haley was engaged with the Anglican mission community in Ruanda-Urundi, and he played a role in the East African Revival, a Holy Spirit-directed movement which Allen must surely have been observing from Nairobi. In Haley, Allen would have found a fellow traveller who profited from his avant-garde work and sought to put it into practice.

Edwin W Smith (1876-1957)

In his section on the devolution from mission to church, Haley makes one, footnoted, reference to the work of Christian

---

78. Shenk, *Changing Frontiers*, 55.
79. Payne, 322.
80. See, for instance, Bishop Lesslie Newbigin's foreword to the 1962 reprint of *Missionary Methods*.

missionary, translator, and anthropologist, Edwin W Smith. On p. 104 Haley speaks of 'serious mistakes' being made when, through ignorance or lack of knowledge "of the customs of the people," indigenous peoples were "provoked to rebellion." He intimates that Smith may be helpful in understanding these issues or provide examples.

Smith was born of Primitive Methodist missionary parents in South Africa. While his parents returned to denominational ministry in Britain when he was still a pre-teen, Smith returned to South Africa in 1898 to pursue a career in bible translation. He spent some time in Lesotho and with a young family, departed in 1902 for Zambia, the same year Haley arrived in Mozambique. In his first term in Zambia, he translated the Gospel of Mark into the Ila language, and wrote a still-respected, *Handbook of the Ila Language* (1907). Smith is regarded as one of "the first scholars to make sustained arguments for the importance of learning African languages and cultures, and for viewing African religions as vehicles of God's grace."[81]

After his second term, following the completion of the Ila New Testament and co-authoring a classic two-volume ethnography *Ila Speaking Peoples of Northern Rhodesia* (only published in 1920), Smith returned to Britain in 1915, where he served with the British and Foreign Bible Society for the rest of his working life. In 1909 he had become a member of Britain's Royal Anthropological Society, and served as its president 1933-35, the only Christian missionary to do so. In 1926 he helped to found the International African Institute.[82] During the 1920s and 30s, Smith played a pivotal role in popularizing the new academic field of African Studies. Following his retirement he lectured in the United

---

81. Dana Robert, 2011, 102.
82. http://www.internationalafricaninstitute.org/about.html (accessed Sept 28, 2011)

States (1939-1944).[83] Over his career, Smith published a wide selection of books on anthropology, African studies, African religion, African Christian theology, and the practice of Christian mission.

In 1926, Smith delivered the Hartley Lecture before the conference of the Primitive Methodist Church, his home denomination. The lecture would be published as *The Golden Stool: some aspects of the conflict of cultures in Africa*. The book cites a conflictual incident in British colonial history set in The Gold Coast (Ghana) where lack of understanding of indigenous culture created a serious backlash. Smith believed that "the form in which Christianity was expressed in any culture should be appropriate to that culture, and he opposed the belief that traditional customs were necessarily wrong. It distressed him that so many believed that one could not be both Christian and African…"[84] Of particular interest to Haley would be Smith's statement: "Missionaries are not a permanent factor in the life of Africa – they will one day (the sooner the better) disappear because no longer needed. It is not their business to decide what form African Christianity shall take."[85]

In 1926, travelling between South Africa and North America, Haley met with British and Foreign Bible Society personnel in London, exploring options for new ministry. It is possible the Haley and Smith actually met during that discussion. If we can assume that Haley had read *The Golden Stool* (there is no direct quote), he would have encountered Smith's profound respect for African people, their languages,

---

83. W John Young, "The Legacy of Edwin W Smith," *International Bulletin of Missionary Research*, Vol 25, (3) 2001, 126-130.
84. Ibid., p.127.
85. Edwin W Smith, *The Golden Stool*, London: Holborn Publishing House, 1926, 281-82.

cultures and religions, and the conviction that Christian faith and community must take root in African forms.

Oswald J Smith (1889-1986)

Haley and his family were home on furlough in Ontario, Canada 1938-40. It seems likely that this is the time period when Haley would have come across the ministry and publications of Oswald J Smith, the pastor of the new non-denominational, The Peoples Church, in Toronto.[86] Haley quotes from Smith's small booklet of collected essays and sermons, *Can Organized Religion Survive?* His extensive quote from Smith on p. 84 of the manuscript focuses attention on "the one and only business of the foreign missionary is to train native workers and put responsibility upon them."[87] In the late 1940s Haley would repeat this statement almost verbatim to his own superiors in the Free Methodist Mission.

Oswald J Smith, like Haley, was a southwestern Ontario farm boy with a call to mission service. Smith served as a pastor within the Presbyterian and Christian and Missionary Alliance Churches in Toronto before planting a new church (1928) in the rented facilities of Massey Hall. While Smith never served overseas as a missionary, besides his role as the founding pastor of The People's Church, he travelled extensively in a preaching ministry that spanned more than 70 countries between 1924 and 1980.[88]

In reference to the Apostle Paul, speaking from his own observed experience, and clearly conversant with the

---

86. The Haley family did not return to Canada during the period 1927-1938, when Smith and The Peoples Church were coming to notice in Toronto.
87. Oswald J Smith, "What's Wrong on the Mission Field?" *Can Organized Religion Survive?* Toronto: Toronto Tabernacle Publishing, 1932, 46-47.
88. "Biography," Papers of Oswald J Smith, Collection 322, Billy Graham Centre Archives, Wheaton, IL, http://www2.wheaton.edu/bgc/archives/GUIDES/322.htm#3 (accessed Nov. 23, 2011).

indigenous church model and the notion of self-support, Smith states: "he (Paul) placed responsibility upon the natives themselves, made the churches founded self-supporting and self-propagating, and that from the very first…please note what I say – self-supporting *from the very first*. For upon that rock, practically all modern missions have gone down…"[89]

Not surprising that Haley found Smith's kindred spirit an encouragement to his developing work in Burundi.

J Merle Davis (1875-1960)

In Haley's manuscript, American IMC mission researcher J Merle Davis is quoted extensively, from two different publications.

Davis was born and raised in Japan, where his parents had been Baptist missionaries (ABCFM) for almost 40 years. After attending Oberlin College in the United States, he returned to Japan (1905) as Secretary of the Nagasaki and then Tokyo YMCAs. On furlough in the USA in 1923-24, Davis became a key figure in the ground-breaking *Survey on Race Relations* on the Pacific Coast, conducted by the Institute of Social and Religious Research, connected with Stanford University, funded by the Rockefeller Foundation (1924-26).[90] One of the goals of this social survey was to reduce anti-Japanese sentiments in California. Following this assignment Davis became General Secretary of the new Institute of Pacific Relations (1926-1929),[91] another body, based in Hawaii, funded by Rockefeller and Carnegie, devoted to reducing East-West tensions.[92]

---

89. Ibid., 45-46.
90. Robert E Park (1864-1944), founder of the original Chicago School of sociology, was also involved in this research project.
91. see http://en.wikipedia.org/wiki/Institute_of_Pacific_Relations (accessed Sept 27, 2011).

In 1929 Davis became Director of the Department of Social and Economic Research and Counsel of the International Missionary Council (IMC), a position he held until his retirement in 1949. Over a 20-year period Davis would conduct numerous research and publishing projects on the African Copperbelt, Indonesia, Latin America and the Caribbean.[93] While Davis was part of a grouping of American Christians with international experience (including John Mott, JH Oldham, etc) often regarded as proponents of the "social gospel,"[94] his sensitivity to cultural differences and advocacy for the capacity of the emerging indigenous churches made an impact upon the development of Haley's mission practice.

Haley's first reference (77) cites the example of the Adventist Mission written up by Davis, in *The Church in the New Jamaica: a study of the economic and social basis of the evangelical church in Jamaica* (1942), a publication of the International Missionary Council (IMC). Haley focuses on the role of missionary input as empowering and providing key resources – a small farm and training school became the basis for a self-supporting, organized, autonomous church. At the time of Davis' publication in 1942, only three expatriates were involved in training, while the work thrived with more than 10,000 members.

Shortly after that section, Haley (78) employs a long quote from Davis to bolster his own argument "that there are no people so poor that they cannot propagate and sustain their

92. Henry Yu, "Professions of Faith: Missionaries, Sociologists and the Survey of Race Relations 1924-26," *Thinking Orientals: Migration, Contact, and Exoticism in Modern America*, New York: Oxford University Press, 2001, 19-30.
93. See *Time* magazine reference regarding his research in Brazil (1943), http://www.time.com/time/magazine/article/0,9171,777871,00.html (accessed Sept 27, 2011).
94. Charles Forman, "J Merle Davis," in Gerald Anderson, *Biographical Dictionary of Christian Missions*, Grand Rapids: Eerdmans, 1999, 171.

Church in their own way." In light of Haley's concern for the nature of the Church and the activity of the Holy Spirit, he seems to be drawing our attention to Davis' comment: "such an assumption is based upon a mistaken concept of the Church and a failure to recognize fully the inner capacity and available resources of races which have a different cultural heritage and economy."[95]

Haley quotes again (80) from Davis' massive compilation prepared for the IMC's Tambaram/Madras, India conference (1938), *The Economic Basis of the Church*. In writing about the attitude of Western missionaries, Haley asks if missionaries, who are aliens, and only emissaries of the Church, have the right "to bind a people by so fusing their western economy with the Gospel they propagate?"

To make his point, Haley quotes from Davis, regarding a young Indian Christian's critique of traditional missionary methods: "Some of us who are products of this system have experienced a revulsion from it and have returned to an Indianized interpretation of religious service. We believe that this is nearer the real spirit of Christ..."[96] This young man was one of Gandhi's lieutenants in the 1930s when Davis interviewed him. When Haley is writing a decade or so later, Gandhi had just recently been assassinated (1948), and we note his respect for the Mahatma's attitude ("he gave the world a glimpse of lowliness, that admittedly, he found in Jesus," 81).

The themes found here regarding the nature of the Church, the inner capacity and resourcefulness of all individuals and cultural communities,[97] and the attitude of the missionary, will be discussed further in Haley's Missiology.

---

95. J Merle Davis, *The Church in the New Jamaica*, London: Oxford University Press, 1942, 31.
96. J Merle Davis (compiled by), *The Economic Basis of the Church*, London: Oxford University Press, 1939, 152.

Other References

Haley cites several other influences, or at least advocates of a similar approach to missionary activity; notably **Bishop Stephen Neill** (1900-1984), Anglican missionary to India from 1928-1944, and on staff of the World Council of Churches from 1947-1954. Neill's address to the International Missionary Council at Whitby in 1947 is referenced in Haley's manuscript.[98] **Frank Laubach** (1884-1970), a missionary to the Philippines who developed a rapid literacy acquisition method,[99] is cited as advocating the notion of "local, unpaid people to teach."[100] Haley even applauds the initiatives of Roman Catholic **Pope Pius XII** (1876-1958), in the formation of three new hierarchies in Africa, thus increasing the possibility of Africans being appointed bishop or archbishop.[101]

What strikes the reader as we make sense of Haley's various influences is their sheer breadth. He was not afraid to glean from the best of input from biblical theology (conservative and mainline), anthropology, social science, and the emerging field of development economics. Despite limited

---

97. The quotes from *Economic Basis* are from a chapter entitled, "The Psychology of Self-Support."
98. *Manuscript*, 77.
99. Laubach, *The Silent Billion Speak*, New York: Friendship Press, 1945.
100. Ibid., 88.
101. Ibid., 86. Haley suggests the Roman Catholic Church is "always ahead in strategy." In a 1944 speech, Pius XII said ""The magnanimous and noble purpose which missionaries have is the propagation of the faith in new lands in such a way that the Church may ever become more firmly established in them and as soon as possible reach such a stage of development that it can continue to exist and flourish without the aid of missionary organizations. These missionary organizations do not serve their own ends, but it is their task to use every endeavour to realize the lofty purpose we have already mentioned. When that has been attained, then let them be happy to turn to other fields." *Address to the Directors of Pontifical Mission Works*, AAS 36 (1944)

formal education Haley was able to read, integrate, experiment with, and advocate for, the most current and erudite missiological thinking of his day, while developing his own ministry construct which, at the end of his career, he introduced and guided in Burundi for a decade before his own retirement.

Haley's Missiology – The Mission Temporary, the Church Permanent

In seeking to develop an overview of Haley's key missiological principles the reader merely has to follow the logic of his outline for the manuscript. The role of the Holy Spirit is central to the initiation and flourishing of Christian communities. The missionary and/or mission team as agent has a key, but limited role. In Haley's view the mission team, as agent, must move on, leaving the Spirit-empowered national leadership to develop appropriate, contextual, organizational practices. As a constant through this whole framework are the practical implications of the encounter between Western missionary and African local economies.

The Role of the Holy Spirit

Haley was not a Pentecostal but he had a profound understanding of the role of the Holy Spirit as active agent of the Trinity, at a time when other conservative evangelicals looked askance at "pentecostal manifestations."[102] In the manuscript he states:

> It is significant that Jesus would not permit his disciples to do anything towards the founding of the Church until the arrival of the Holy Spirit, "the promise of the Father." This was not alone that they might be prepared by tarrying, important as that was, but the Holy Spirit, who proceedeth from the Father and the Son, is their Executive during the church dispensation and only He could be entrusted with so important a matter as building the body of Christ.[103]

Haley believed that spiritual gifts are dispersed by the Holy Spirit for the purpose of building the church, not for personal ministry or gain. "How near we may be to grieving Him, when we thoughtlessly speak of 'my work, my schools, my teachers, my evangelists,' or lightly of any of the gifts He (the Holy Spirit) has received from Jesus with which to enable the Church in her conflict with the world."[104]

Following an overview of New Testament evangelists empowered by the Holy Spirit (Peter, Philip, Paul), Haley suggests that it was because of this "divine pattern" – spiritual gifts and enablements being given and fully directed by the Holy Spirit – that the early churches were so quickly able to pass on leadership responsibilities to local, indigenous leadership. "Even those who were unlearned and ignorant, former idolaters and slaves, with these enablements of the

102. Haley references his use of the Scofield Study Bible, an interpretive framework suggesting that the dramatic gifts of the Holy Spirit have ceased; but does not go in that direction himself: "in speaking of the gifts of the Holy Spirit, to the Church, whether they have ceased or not, we are on holy ground and holy men remove their shoes," *Manuscript*, 69.
103. Ibid., 63.
104. Ibid., 65.

Holy Spirit, did then, and have since, when permitted to do so, carried forward devotedly the work of God."[105]

Haley was convinced that if new believers, in any cultural context, were gifted and empowered by the Holy Spirit, they would be led into truth and guided in the development of their organizational life, without the oversight of missionary personnel.

The Role of the Missionary

In a number of different places Haley articulated a strong perspective on the task of the missionary. "Evangelical missionaries should be especially committed to the developing of a holy, taught ministry for the Church that God the Holy Spirit builds."[106] Preaching the gospel and the receiving of new converts was a "laboratory" for the empowerment of the Holy Spirit. Gifted preachers and pastors would emerge and the missionary's task was to train, provide active apprenticeship opportunities, including correction and further teaching, and the opportunity to be tested in the midst of adversity. Haley felt "we leave the New Testament pattern when we usurp their place as pastors and confine them to the place of helpers and servants and that for decades or a century."[107]

During Haley's retirement the Free Methodist mission community, within which he served, was conducting a series of missionary seminars in the period 1946-50. As a senior missionary practitioner, Haley contributed to these seminars:

> "Our work is to build the church; to train for it pastors and teachers, ordaining elders, and to make

---

105. Ibid., 72.
106. Ibid., 83.
107. Ibid., 72.

the period of tutelage as short as possible…it is the right of the people of any country to carry the gospel to their own people. We go to show them the way. By giving too much money we deprive the people of the privilege of doing what they should for the kingdom. Self-support, self-government, and self-propagation are a unit and indivisible."[108]

Haley likened the emergence of a national church leadership community to that of a family. It is understood that the children will eventually grow to a place where they are entrusted with responsibilities and participate in the family councils. And then, quite naturally they will pick up and carry on with life in their own right. "The Church increases and the mission decreases. There are no throes of devolution, for all this was foreseen and planned, as in the case of a wise and loving family."[109]

At this point, in Haley's view, the missionary would pick up and move on to the next setting where the gospel was still yet to be preached.

The Interplay of Church and Mission

In his writing, as well as in his practice, Haley expressed impatience with a church that trained missionaries and set up mission stations in unreached lands while achieving a "paucity of results" when compared with the early, apostolic Church.[110] In his opinion, the situation called for "a comprehensive study and an intensive examination of methods with a view to the elimination of fruitless ones."[111]

---

108. in Lamson, *Tide*, 24.
109. Op cit., 76.
110. Haley, *Manuscript*, 62.
111. Ibid.

Haley speaks of the Church as God's instrument of redemption, as an agent in God's purposes for the world. The Holy Spirit is the key motivator in building the Church, and the Spirit gives gifts to the Body of Christ to enable the accomplishment of God's mission. The purpose of "the mission" (as Haley used the term; the task team or sent-out agent), is to plant churches through, primarily, preaching and foundational discipling. From that point onward the Holy Spirit would take the initiative, guiding into truth, enabling the fruit of the Spirit, distributing the gifts of the Spirit.[112]

The forms that a church will take in a particular context should be the initiative of the Holy Spirit, suggested Haley, citing Ephesians 2:21-22. The "mission" may point toward the simpler forms of church organization initially. The "missionaries" may serve at the direction of church leadership until such a time as they move on to another location. Haley indicated that "the Church increases and the mission decreases." Again, Haley is here referring to "the mission" as a task team or sent-out agent.[113]

Haley sought to put in practice the following principle: "the mission, from the beginning, should foresee its own retirement and institute nothing that the young Church will not be able to carry, eventually."[114] He cites Bishop Stephen Neill speaking at the 1947 International Missionary Council meetings in Whitby, Ontario:

> From the beginning of an evangelistic task in a new area, the aim must be the bringing into existence at the earliest possible date of a self-governing and self-propagating Church and every effort must be

---

112. Haley cites key scripture passages as rationale: 1 Cor 1:21, 6:9-11, 12:8-11, 12:27-28; Eph. 4:12-13; 1 Pet 2:5; Ibid., 66-67.
113. Ibid., 76.
114. Ibid., 77.

made to make the period of tutelage as short as possible.[115]

It is in this sense that Haley speaks of "the mission temporary – the church permanent."[116]

Capacity of Indigenous Leadership

Haley was convinced of the role of the Holy Spirit in developing leadership capacity in any new believer, regardless of racial or cultural background, confirming Allen's insight:

> If we have no faith in the power of the Holy Spirit in them, they will not learn to have faith in the power of the Holy Spirit in themselves… trust which begets trustworthiness, is the one essential for any success in the Pauline method.[117]

Haley cites his own heritage within the Methodist community when he speaks of the role of common lay workers as the backbone of the movement. The preachers, evangelists and trained clergy, such as Wesley himself, opened up new areas while local lay ministers gave their attention to "constant, prayerful care, house-to-house visitation, seeking the lost, sick and straying, consolidating and maintaining gains."[118] From his own experience as a pioneer Free Methodist church planter in Saskatchewan, he had reflected on the role of the apostolic worker in relation to the development of self-propagating local congregations. Haley was convinced that "such a system will work on mission fields, even among peoples of a

---

115. Stephen C Neill, "The Church in a Revolutionary World," *International Review of Mission*, V36:4 (October 1947): 434-451.
116. Haley, *Manuscript*, 72.
117. Allen, *Missionary Methods*, 152.
118. Haley, *Manuscript*, 79.

subsistence economy. Let them build their church buildings and schools when they feel the need, according to their own economy."[119]

A long quote in his manuscript, from Davis, bolsters Haley's own argument "that there are no people so poor that they cannot propagate and sustain their Church in their own way." In light of Haley's concern for the nature of the Church and the activity of the Holy Spirit, he seems to be drawing our attention to Davis' comment: "such an assumption [that poor Africans cannot manage without the missionaries] is based upon a mistaken concept of the Church and a failure to recognize fully the inner capacity and available resources of races which have a different cultural heritage and economy."[120]

When Haley retired from Burundi in 1946, the policy and practice required for developing indigenous churches was obviously still on his mind, as his work on this manuscript attests. In a letter to Bishop Ormiston of The Free Methodist Church (USA) in 1948 he wrote: "…the young churches are becoming self-conscious. Like the son in the home they should be welcomed into our councils. To delay too long might be costly."[121]

African-Initiated Churches (AICs)

In Chapter 10 Haley engages in a discussion of what today are referred to as African Initiated Churches. Haley uses the language of his day referring to them as "prophet movements." There is no question that Haley is viewing these movements as a point upon a continuum with other

---

119. Ibid., 80.
120. J Merle Davis, *The Church in the New Jamaica*, London: Oxford University Press, 1942, 31.
121. Haley in Lamson, *Tide*, Preface, i.

expressions of Christianity. He doesn't place himself with other Western missionaries who express fear and desire to suppress these indigenous Christians. Neither is he completely at ease. Haley suggests these movements "believe they are led of God, and we would be prepared to grant that, were it not that there is so much in the movement that seems foreign to the Gospel."[122]

Pentecostal researcher, Allan Anderson supplies some background: "Following the European colonization of Africa during the nineteenth century, a process of religious acculturation took place as older African religious and social traditions were threatened and partially replaced by new ones. The independent African Christian churches that began to emerge at the turn of the twentieth century were initially snubbed. Western mission church leaders and other observers dismissed them as sects and labeled them "nativistic," "messianic," "separatist," and "syncretistic."[123]

Haley would have been well-acquainted with the Zionist AIC churches in South Africa founded by Daniel Nkonyane (1910) and Isaiah Shembe (1911). At the time of writing he may have recently read Swedish missionary and IMC researcher Bengt Sundkler's seminal book on AICs, *Bantu Prophets in South Africa* (1948).[124] Haley's comments in the manuscript suggest ambivalence – there is much good, and some that is suspicious. It was the principle of indigenous development that appealed to him. He may have resonated with Anderson's current assessment of these movements: "The AICs offer living, radical experiments of an indigenized

---

122. *Manuscript*, 106.
123. Allan Anderson, "Types and Butterflies: African Initiated Churches and European Typologies," *International Bulletin of Missionary Research*, July 2001, 108.
124. Bengt G W Sundkler, *Bantu Prophets in South Africa*, Oxford: Oxford University Press, 1948.

Christianity that has consciously rejected Western ecclesiastical models and forms of being Christian."[125]

Toward the end of Chapter 10, Haley refers to the Balakole Revival emerging in East Africa during the 1930s-40s. In one breath he wonders if this is similar to other AIC developments, while in another he feels there is something different.

The Balakole Revival was birthed within the Anglican Church in Uganda as an internal critique, but it quickly spread to other regions and other Protestant Churches. "It largely remained within these churches, both because of the revivalist's reluctance to create separatist churches and because the Revival message had limited appeal to the burgeoning African independent churches."[126]

As already noted, Haley's perspective seems to have swayed the concerns of Anglican missionaries in Burundi regarding this new "revival." He viewed it as genuine action of the Holy Spirit and resonates with Anglican missionary A C Stanley Smith's comment that, in fact, the revival is having the biggest influence on "drawing together white and black."[127]

Missions and Money

Although self-aware regarding the place of white, Western, influence on the development of indigenous church practices, Haley's primary reflections regarding financial matters focused on his concern for the development of self-sustaining

---

125. Anderson, 108.
126. Emma Wild-Wood, "The East African Revival in the Study of African Christianity," *The East African Revival: History and Legacies*, Kevin Ward, Emma Wild-Wood (editors), Farnham, UK: Ashgate Publications, 2012, 201.
127. *Manuscript*, 108.

Christian community – at the level that the local economy could support.

Along with multiple references throughout the text, Haley has a short chapter (VII) focused on "Finance." His opening salvo: "to fail to give the young Church a sound, workable plan could keep it in economic bondage to the mission indefinitely."[128] In his case in Burundi, "the mission had definitely stated that it would neither give nor loan money for the salaries of the Pastor-Teachers. They were the responsibility of the Church."[129] In fact, Haley felt it almost impossible for a missionary to 'dispense' funds to national pastors without the 'master-servant' image arising – "a relationship entirely foreign to an equal brotherhood."[130]

Recognizing that, in many instances, mission organizations had already implemented systems of paid national evangelists/pastors, Haley advocated starting anew, with outright confession to national leadership that the mission had followed unsatisfactory, man-made methods, not having "sought out the order of the Acts and Epistles, which were written for our instruction and guidance."[131] Having accepted responsibility for unsatisfactory work already done, "we could humbly propose to our people that we now desire to study, with them, the Scriptural plan."[132]

In his own lived experience, Haley had participated in a system in Southern Africa where paid pastor-teachers were the norm. He had observed pastors become 'well-to-do" in their local economies and parishioners coming to beg from them. He knew this methodology would never build an indigenous church. Hence, his implementation of an

---

128. Ibid., 91.
129. Ibid., 92.
130. Ibid., 94.
131. Ibid., 100.
132. Ibid.

indigenous approach – "from the start" – as he moved to Burundi.

While not wanting to minimize the significance of the interplay between Western colonization and missionary activity, Haley's goal was that the missionary's initial role as evangelist should be soon replaced by discipled and trained national leadership, who would continue the ongoing development of the work, while the missionary moved on to another unreached location. The intention was thus to minimize the Western missionary's economic and social impact upon the local economy.

"Indigenous" Today?

John Wesley Haley wrote the document we are examining more than 60 years ago. In his early life, he was the product of 19th century, rural, Canadian life, motivated by a revivalistic Free Methodist theology and practice. By the time of his writing, however, he had lived for more than 35 years in Africa, engaged with early 20th century colonial politics, interacted with a rich missiological literature, and learned from, as well as contributed to, a wide-ranging, ecumenical missionary community. So what does Haley have to offer for our consideration in the early 21st century?

In describing the progress of evangelical mission methodology over the past century, Wilbert Shenk speaks of three models – replication, indigenization and contextualization.

In the *replication* model, "Mission is a process through which the missionary seeks to replicate or reproduce a church in another culture patterned after that of the church from which the missionary originated. The missionary as a representative of Christendom is charged with responsibility for the success of the outcome."[133] Much of evangelical mission in the 20th century followed this approach. This is the very model that Haley struggled to overcome.

On the other hand, "*Indigenization* emphasized finding the functional equivalent within the other culture for the 'original.' That is to say, the goal of indigenization was to find the symbols and forms in the host culture through which the Christendom view of religious life might be expressed."[134] The script is still provided from outside, but a differentiated view of culture is assumed as well as the notion that culture is evolving. Shenk indicates that Allen took the indigenization argument of Venn and Anderson to a new level; "Allen did not propose a new theory of culture, but he argued that the church can take root in every cultural context and there become a faithful representation of the body of Christ."[135] Allen and Haley had an intuitive vision for what an emergent indigenous church should look like. The question is, did their suggested practices for indigenization point toward that intuitive vision?

A third mission model to emerge from the early 1970s onwards, influenced particularly by Catholic mission practice, was that of *contextualization*. Shenk describes this as "a process whereby the gospel message encounters a particular culture, calling forth faith and leading to the formation of a faith community, which is culturally authentic and authentically Christian. Control of the process resides within the context rather than with an external agent or agency."[136]

My reading of Haley's missiology in this manuscript would suggest that his approach, infused with the full presence of the Trinity, was closer to the contextualization approach, even though he only had 'indigenization' language

133. Shenk, *Changing Frontiers*, 51
134. Ibid., 55
135. Ibid., 55
136. Ibid., 56.

to use at the time. Again Shenk suggests that in the contextualization model, "the missionary's task is to be an instrument of ongoing transformation in the world. If the missionary's being and work are to be an instrument, this suggests that someone else is in control."[137] Haley would suggest that 'someone else' is in fact the Holy Spirit.

And so the learning, reflection, and recasting of the mission task continues. Current thinking and practice in a globalized, multicultural world calls for *incarnational*, worshipping communities modeled by intercultural mission teams, moving beyond the 'us-them' paradigm.[138] Likewise, the 'dependency' conversation continues to absorb much effort from missiologists.[139]

John Wesley Haley – A Wesleyan Missionary

Haley, throughout his missionary career, was firmly rooted in the Wesleyan/Free Methodist world of theology and practice. In the past decade, Free Methodist mission leaders have fleshed out an overview of distinctively Wesleyan leadership qualities.[140] Haley is a primary exemplar of these qualities. He was noted by colleagues as grace-filled and disciplined in

---

137. Ibid., 58.
138. See Newbigin, *The Gospel in a Pluralist Society*, Eerdmans, 1989; Cray, *Mission-Shaped Church*, Church Publishing House, 2004; Stone, *Evangelism After Christendom*, Abingdon, 2007.
139. See Corbett and Fikkert, *When Helping Hurts*, Moody, 2009; Rowell, *To Give or Not to Give*, Authentic, 2007; Reese, *Roots & Remedies of the Dependency Syndrome in World Missions*, William Carey Library, 2010; Rickett, *Building Strategic Relationships*, Stem Press, 2008. A very helpful article in this conversation can be found by Robert Reese, "Western Missions and Dependency," *Missio Dei: A Journal of Missional Theology and Praxis*, 2.2 August 2011, 59-72. http://missiodeijournal.com/md-2-2/81 (downloaded September 11, 2012).
140. "Developing Leaders: Principles for Free Methodist World Missions," in

his spiritual life. He exhibited a certain catholicity of spirit in the breadth of his appreciation for Christian traditions far afield of his own. The exercise of Christian ministry naturally overflowed in wholistic concern for the social, educational and medical needs of the people among whom his family lived. Haley remained connected to the fellowship of his own denomination as well as the wider ecumenical Christian community, never becoming isolated, sectarian or parochial. Finally, his continual emphasis on allowing the Holy Spirit to empower the whole priesthood of believers places Haley firmly within a Wesleyan expression.[141]

In fact, after reading Haley's manuscript, we can almost imagine his hearty affirmation of this statement from Free Methodist mission theologian Howard Snyder:

> Wesley's stress on preceding grace and on the power of the Holy Spirit to perfect Christian character suggests an optimism of grace that should infuse our church planting and discipling. If God can transform people into the likeness of Jesus Christ, he can build communities that transcend racial, ethnic, socioeconomic, and cultural differences.[142]

Dan Sheffield (ed.) *A Theology of Mission for Free Methodist World Missions*, 2nd edition, Indianapolis: FMWM, 2006, 17-18.

141. In commenting on Acts 15:28, "it seemed good to the Holy Spirit and to us," Wesleyan scholar and missiologist, Dean Flemming indicates, "This suggests both divine and human participation in the theological process. But the order of the words implies that the will of the Spirit is paramount. The Spirit brings discernment to a Christian community in theological dialogue. Presumably, this guidance involves recognizing God's genuine activity in the lives of others, as well as grasping how Scripture speaks to the situation." "Contextualization in a Wesleyan Spirit," in Darrell Whiteman and Gerald Anderson (eds.), *World Mission in the Wesleyan Spirit*, Franklin, Tenn: Providence House Publishers, 2009, 21.

Upon Haley's death, in 1951, Ron Collett, a fellow Canadian missionary colleague, had this to say:

> "He did not spare himself in his effort to establish an indigenous church ... which had been the ideal for so many years. Nor was his extent of influence confined to his own denomination in this respect. It is safe to say that the other missions in Ruanda-Urundi received their first lessons in indigenous church principles from him. In this matter alone he has rendered a lasting service to other missions in the country. He himself never fully realized to what extent indigenous church principles have been adopted by the other missions."[143]

As recently as a decade ago, Bishop Gerald Bates, who had worked as a missionary in Burundi following Haley's passing, commented:

> "Haley always built carefully. He learned to make burnt bricks and tiles so that his buildings would withstand the assaults of tropical storms. He worked with equal care in forming a self-supporting, self-propagating church, built on principles of stewardship and national leader development."[144]

The legacy of Haley's determined endeavour in Burundi lives on with the Free Methodist church community, presently numbering more than 948 congregations and a membership of

---

142. Snyder, "What's Unique About a Wesleyan Theology of Mission?" in Sheffield, *A Theology of Mission,* 26.
143. "In Memoriam, A Prince in Israel," *The Missionary Tidings,* April 1951.
144. "John Wesley Haley, Prophet and Apostle," *Free Methodist Historical Society Newsletter,* Summer 2001, Vol. 2, No. 1.

155,207, besides adherents.[145] When Haley died in 1951, the Free Methodist-affiliated believers in Burundi, were 2282. A decade before, in 1941, as Haley was laying the indigenous foundation "from the start" there were only 163 members. This represents a growth rate of 1300% over ten years, or an annual growth rate of 130%.[146]

---

145. http://fmcusa.org/fmwm/countries/burundi/ (accessed Jan 11, 2012)
146. Hohensee, *Burundi*, 139.

Notes on Haley's Journal

At the beginning of his *Journal*, Haley states that, "the South African Diaries I have been using are not satisfactory, as the space given is often too small, and some days I do not care to write. The space for Sundays is very small. So I bought this book today."[1] It appears that "this book" and others that he continued to use were what we would call school workbooks or scribblers.

The journals are written in a beautiful cursive script, with veryfew strike-overs or corrections. Spelling and grammar are of a well-educated man. At one point, there is a little

1. *Journal*, 2.

creation at the side of the page that Haley identifies as "Florence's kitty." The *Journal* is, in fact, a wonderful human history of his work as a missionary.

Haley's practice was to write, sometimes almost daily, but more often in fairly large chunks at the end of several days or weeks. This may reflect the demands for more physical work or ministry, or may indicate that conditions were not favourable to writing – this could well have been the case at the end of his 17 hour long days in Saskatchewan when tired and having only a kerosene lantern to light his work. At one point, he seems to write a second body of material for a date for which he had written other material. This writer has attempted to date those pages appropriately.

Great detail attends his record of attempts to be the peace-maker counsellor when he was charged with the presidency of the conference in South Africa. He anguished over the feelings of others, and sought meetings with those in need to counsel and pray with them. The needs, health, and concerns of his wife are often noted. Many entries deal with his concerns for the schooling of his children. His disappointment that his son Blake has not joined him in his mission work surfaces again and again.

Some of the pages pose difficulties in understanding because his pen was giving out. His dating is sometimes challenging. Sometimes a date will be 3rd, another time Mar. 3rd, another, Thurs. March 3rd, 1924. When pages go on for several with the briefer notations, it is sometimes difficult to get the date right.

In order to make reference to entries in the *Journal* more identifiable, and to prevent disaster if all of the 744 loose pages were to spill, we have attempted to date and number pages in a usable manner. Approximately 220 words are included on each page.

Burton. W. Hamilton

Select Bibliography

Allan, David. *From the Lumber Camp to the Ministry*. Toronto: Evangelical Publishers, 1938.

Allen, Roland. *Missionary Methods: St Paul's or Ours?* Grand Rapids: Eerdmans, 1962.

Bates, Gerald, *Soul Afire: Life of J. W. Haley*. Indianapolis: Light and Life Press, 1993.

Bates, Gerald, "John Wesley Haley: Prophet and Apostle." *Free Methodist Historical Society Newsletter*, Summer 2001, Vol. 2, No.1

Bates, Gerald, *J. W. Haley: Blazing African Trails*. Indianapolis, Indiana: Light and Life, February, 1993.

Guillebaud, Meg. *Rwanda, the Land God Forgot? Revival, Genocide and Hope*. London: Monarch Books, 2002.

Haley, J. W., *The Journal of J. W. Haley*. a hand-written document of 477 pages found in the 1970's in a termite-ridden attic in Burundi, 1924 – 1938. The original is located in the Archives of Spring Arbor University, Michigan. Susan Panak, Archivist, has been an indefatigable source of information, including the copying of the Haley *Journal* and copies of relative materials from *The Missionary Tidings*.

Haley, J. W., *But Thy Right Hand*. Winona Lake, IN: Light and Life Press, 1949.

Haley, J. W. "Building the Indigenous Church in Mid-Africa." *United Evangelical Action*, Vol 8 (13), August 15, 1949.

Haley, J. W., *But Thy Right Hand*. World Mission People, a précis of the book by Danial V. Runyon, November/December, 1996.

Haley, J. W. & Haley, Jennie, *Congo – Nile Notes, No. 9*. Haleys' submission typed on onion-skin paper for publication in this semi-monthly report to the home sending countries, July 1936.

Haley, J. W., *Life in Mozambique and South Africa*. Chicago: Free Methodist Publishing House, 1926.

Haley, Hodges & Soltau and others, *The Indigenous Church: The Biblical Method of Missions*. Lectures given at the EFMA Annual Convention, Chicago, Illinois, 1949.

Hohensee, Donald. *Church Growth in Burundi*. Pasadena, CA: William Carey Library, 1977.

Hogue, Wilson T. *The History of the Free Methodist Church of North America* (Vol. II). Chicago: Free Methodist Publishing House, 1915.

Lamson, Byron. *To Catch the Tide*. Winona Lake, IN: General Missionary Board, 1963.

Metaxas, Eric. *Bonhoeffer: Pastor, Martyr, Prophet, Spy*. Nashville: Thomas Nelson Publishing, 2010.

Sigsworth, John. W., *The Battle Was The Lord's*. Sage Publishers, Oshawa, Ontario, 1960.

Weisberger, Bernard A. *They Gathered at the River*. Boston: Little, Brown and Co. 1958.

_____, ed, "In Memoriam – A Prince in Israel." *The Missionary Tidings April*. Winona Lake, Indiana 1951.

_____, ed, "In Memoriam – A True Missionary Mother." *The Missionary Tidings*. Winona Lake, Indiana, 1952.

_____, ed, *The Missionary Tidings*. reference has been made to many copies of this journal, some written by Haley, others about him and the work in Central Africa, 1938 – 1951, Winona Lake, Indiana.

www.ingramcontent.com/pod-product-compliance
Ingram Content Group UK Ltd.
Pitfield, Milton Keynes, MK11 3LW, UK
UKHW041303180426
11947UKWH00009B/652